Poetic Possibilities

Poetic Possibilities

An Original Collection Showing the Moving, Innovative, and Positive Potential of Poetry and How to Write It

Bartholomew Williams

RESOURCE *Publications* • Eugene, Oregon

POETIC POSSIBILITIES
An Original Collection Showing the Moving, Innovative, and Positive Potential of Poetry and How to Write It

Copyright © 2019 Bartholomew Williams. All rights reserved. Except for brief quotations in critical publications or reviews, no part of this book may be reproduced in any manner without prior written permission from the publisher. Write: Permissions, Wipf and Stock Publishers, 199 W. 8th Ave., Suite 3, Eugene, OR 97401.

Resource Publications
An Imprint of Wipf and Stock Publishers
199 W. 8th Ave., Suite 3
Eugene, OR 97401

www.wipfandstock.com

PAPERBACK ISBN: 978-1-5326-8456-2
HARDCOVER ISBN: 978-1-5326-8457-9
EBOOK ISBN: 978-1-5326-8458-6

Manufactured in the U.S.A.   AUGUST 15, 2019

Contents

Acknowledgments | ix
Introduction | xiii

Chapter 1—Inspirational, Nature, and/or Relationship Poetry | 1

You Can Do It! | 3
Dare to Dream! | 4
You Are Worth It | 5
To Uplift, or Live Adrift? | 6
Tell Them Now | 7
ABC's of Appreciation | 8
Building Connections | 10
Looking to Sea | 11
Sunrise! | 12
My Inner Voice—
Supportive Choice | 13
Stargazing Reflections | 14
Rhythm of the Rain | 15
Solitude in Academia | 16
Freedom | 18
Freedom in Flight | 19
Soaring Symbol of Strength | 21
Patriotic Pursuits | 22
Mother | 23
Father | 25
To Be with Her | 26
Beth | 27
Holly | 28
Grandma | 29
Family Farm | 30
Across States, Similar Fates | 32
Sunshine Café | 33
Silently Seeking
Nature's Voice | 34
Connecting with Nature | 35
Time | 36
Glaciers are Weeping | 37
Sometimes | 39
Framework of the Forest | 40
Giant Sequoia—
King of All Trees! | 41
An Eagle Goes Fishing | 42

v

Contents

Chapter 2—Brand New, Innovative Forms of Poetry | 43

The Promise of Spring | 47
Summer's Allure and Time to Mature | 49
Autumn Harvest and Last Call of Fall | 51
Winter Dormancy, Death, and Deliverance | 53
Liquid Life | 55
Skies Raining, Fields Draining | 56
Rivers' Motions Refill Oceans | 57
Childhood: Rising Up, Sizing Up | 58
Young Adulthood: Finding One's Path | 59
Early Middle Age: Calling, Career, and Clan | 60
Late Middle Age: Children Take Flight, a Second Light | 61
Elderly/Golden Age: Time for Shedding Some Tears, but Still Meaningful Years | 62
Books | 63
Fish | 64
Flag | 65
Decades of Distraction | 66
Deliverance at Dunkirk | 67

Friends for Different Ends | 68
Zest to Travel the 50 States of America | 69
Some Rare Matters | 71
Ships and Boats from Z to A | 73
Carnival | 75
Games and Sports | 76
Volunteers | 77
Baseball—Good Call! | 78
Leave it out There | 80
Creative Desire | 81
Willingness to Teach | 82
Drive-in Movie Memories | 83
The Allure of Lighthouses | 85
Admiring Heavenly Bodies | 87
Storms Around the World | 90

Chapter 3—Different Approaches to Writing Poetry | 93

Sarah | 98
Stan | 99
Ready for the Road | 99
Fair Thrills | 100
A Form of Poetry that Uses ABC | 101
Rhyme Time | 102
Lighten Up | 102
Poem Could Be an Etheree | 103

Contents

Chapter 4—Mixing it up— a Variety of Poetry | 107

Seasick | 109
A Taxing Experience | 110
Up and Down, Round and Round | 112
Temporary Space, Personal Place | 113
What am I? | 114
Roll to Play | 115
Gaining Ground | 116
Elusive Poet | 117
A Hot Date | 118
An Eyebrow-raising Key to Electricity | 119
Supersonic! | 120
A Birthday Card | 122
Community Creek | 123
Sudden Storm | 124
Root Beer River | 126
Camping Trip | 128
Road Trips | 130
Stars' Sharing | 131
Tree | 132
Subtle Call of Waterfall | 133
Farms | 134
Maritime Missions | 135
'Sailing' in Space to a Lunar Landing | 138
Ignoring a Warning Left a Nation in Mourning | 140
Titanic Tragedy | 142

POW's Paradox | 144
Lament from the Living | 145
Fear | 146
Still a Brave New World Ahead— Cloning, Eugenics Not Dead? | 147
Some Simple Joys | 149
The Chill of Autumn, the Warmth of Romance | 150
Holistic | 151
Innovation | 152
Willpower | 153
Inquisitiveness | 154
Careful Concerning Contracts | 155
Free—Basic to First Amendment | 156
Where Have Good Manners Gone? | 157
Could Have Rhymed but Doesn't | 158
Some of Life's Phases— In a Few Phrases | 159
Recreational Retreat | 160
Canadian Geese: Still Roam or Stay Home? | 161
Final Footle | 162

Chapter 5—Around the World | 163

Arctic Sustenance | 165
Antarctica— Cold, High, and Dry | 166
Northern Necessities | 167

Contents

Aesthetic Africa | 168
A Wonder Down Under | 169
The Southern Tier of Western Hemisphere | 170
Less Costs More at the Store | 171
One Ancient Wall Stands Above All | 172
Cosmic Context | 173
Living Gratefully | 174
Terrestrial Travels | 175
Sleek, Smart and Social Swimmers | 176
Taught through Trails | 177
New Approaches | 178
"Rubbernecks" in Action Cause Us More Distraction | 179

Chapter 6—Resources and Support | 181

Resources (websites): | 181
Support (books): | 186

Selected Glossary | 189
Index of Titles | 211
Index of First Lines | 217
About the Frontispiece Photos | 222
Bibliography | 223

Acknowledgments

WRITING A BOOK IS a creative and challenging process. Writing your first book is particularly so. I was happy and humbled to learn more about the subject matter while gaining further insight into myself. I am thankful for and acknowledge the help of many people in different ways and on many levels during the creation, research, writing, editing, revising, and publishing of this book.

To my wife, Jodi, and our family, I will always love you with all my heart. Thank you very much for your love, care, support, and understanding through the years. I see the beauty in each of you every day and sincerely appreciate you. Please remember always how dear you are to me.

To my late mother, Irene Williams, I love and thank you for everything you did for me. I especially appreciate the values you taught me. You were always there for me. To my late father, Ken Williams, I love you, too, and thank you for all the good times and memories.

To my late fraternal grandparents, Evan & Regina Williams, thank you so much for your love, kindness, patience, and support. All those weeks spent with you on the farm and elsewhere through the years truly helped shape who I am.

Earl and Charlotte Steinkraus, you have been with me throughout my life, in spirit and every other way. Thank you for sharing yourselves with my family and me. We all love you and your family.

Acknowledgments

Bill & Betty McFarland, Jim, Bill Jr., Betsy, and Michael, and your families, thank you for embodying academic inspiration balanced against real-world practicalities. Your 30-plus years of friendship, help, love, and support say it all. I truly appreciate you.

Dave & Kathy, thank you always for your unwavering love, kindness, and support—now and forever. I am truly grateful for knowing you.

Sister Valerie, Tom Rondeau, Craig Streff, Cynthia Bartz, Mal Dodds, James Gilbert, Dale Hidde, Pat Kirby, Christine Plath, Gerald Swenson, Sam Waala, Charles W. Calomiris, Robert J. Gordon, Philip A. Schrodt, Paul Kimmel, the late Robert Eisner, the late Anna Gossel, the late Mary Alice Hendershot, and many other teachers and professors who gave of their time and talent, I value and respect your knowledge, teaching, and mentoring. You helped me learn how to think critically, consider the many sides of every issue, and articulate my position. I consider myself a lifelong learner, in large part, due to your guidance.

Abraham, Adam, Agnes K., Alexis, Al, Al & Ann, Albert B., Albert E., Alicia, Andrea D., Andrew, Andy & Janet and family, Anne-Lise, Ann & family, Arthur, Arthur R., Barry & Mary and family, Ben, Benjamin, Bernice & Herb, Beth & Scott and family, Bob, Brad D., Bruce, Bruce & Dorothy, Bryan B., Carol C., Carole, Carolyn Devonshire, Charles & Kelly and family, Charles K., Cherry, Connie M., Crystal, Dan & Shirley and family, Dave & Mary and family, Dave A. and family, David, Derek, Don, Don & Sue and family, Dorothy & Phil and family, Doug, Duey, Ed & Sally and family, Edmund, Elaine G., Elizabeth, Elizabeth E., Eric Heiden, Erik & family, Ernest, Eve R., Florence, Frank & Verna, Frankie, Franklin James and family, Friedrich, Gary W., George P., George W., Glenn F., Glenn G., Gloria, Gordon, Gouverneur, Gregory B., Gretchen & Ray, Harro, Helen, Henry, Holly, Isaac, Isaac & Janet, Isaak, Jacob, James, Jan, Jan A., Jason & Jennie and family, Jay & Tanya, Jean M., Jeff, Jennifer, Jennifer E., Jesse, Jesse K. and family, Jill, Jim, Jim & Anne, Jim & Faye, Jim & Ginny and family, Jimi, Jimmy, Joan, Job, Joe & Edna, Joel & Carol, John, John & Donna, John H., José & Mabel and family, Joseph, Joyce J.,

Acknowledgments

Judy, Karen, Karl E., Kathryne & Garth, Katie, Ken, Ken & Sharon, Kim, Kim R., Kristina & Tony and family, Larry, Laura, Laura L., Leonard, Leonardo, Line G., Loretta, Lou, Lucille, Luke, Marcel & Gertrude, Mark, Martha, Mary, Matthew, Maura, Max S., Michael, Michael Akers, Mike, Milton & Rose, Monte & Eileen and family, Nancy, the late Nancy & Alan Miller, Nathan, Noah, Oskar S., Owen & family, Patricia, Patrick, Paul, Peggy, Peter, Randy, Randy & Deanne, Ray D., Robert, Roland & family, Ron & Sandy & family, Ron K., Ronald, Samuel, Samuel C., Scott, Stephen, Steve, Steve & family, Susan A., Susan G., Ted N. & family, Ted & Sue and family, Terry, Theodore, Thomas, Thomas J., Thomas S., Tim, Tim & Jodi and family, Tom, Tom & Dee, Trish, Victor, Virginia, Warren, Wasiliki, William M., William S., William H. S., Winston, and too many others to list here—thank you very much for your friendship and/or inspiration. Each of you has helped me become a better person.

Thank you very much to all U.S. veterans since the birth of our nation. Let us always remember their service, honor their memories, and earn their sacrifices.

Last, but certainly not least, I sincerely thank all the staff members at Wipf and Stock Publishers who believed in my book and helped me make it a reality.

Bartholomew (Bart) Williams
2019

Introduction

"There comes a point in your life when you need to stop reading other people's books and write your own."
—QUOTE WIDELY ATTRIBUTED TO ALBERT EINSTEIN

MINDFUL OF THIS EINSTEIN quote, I wondered if I could generate the creative energy (some call this inspiration; others refer to it as practicing and honing the craft of writing poetry), motivation, research, self-discipline, and determination to write and publish an original book of poetry. I feel fortunate and humbled to have answered that question with this original collection of 132 poems. It covers 60 different primary types of poetry, which I believe show the informative, moving, innovative, and positive power of poetry and different approaches to writing it. This volume was not intended to be an exhaustive set of examples of all the hundreds of forms of poetry. Rather, it is meant to illustrate dozens of different forms of poetry and suggest poetic possibilities, both in terms of using existing forms and creating new ones.

To that end, this book is organized into the following six main sections:

1. Inspirational, Nature, and/or Relationship Poetry. These are fairly self-explanatory. I am deeply interested in and care about principles, people, and our planet, among other

Introduction

concerns. The 34 poems in this section collectively address each of these types of topics.

2. Brand New, Innovative Forms of Poetry. These 32 poems in total account for 11 innovative/new forms of poetry I invented, namely:

- Serial: This is a series of three or more rhyming poems, each of which can stand alone, but as a combined series, tell one larger story. Also, there is a separate overall title for each series of poems that ties the series together.
- Acrostcrete: This is a hybrid of an acrostic and a concrete rhyming poem.
- Deca: This is a rhyming poem consisting of 10 total lines, each with 10 syllables, and no more than five stanzas in which every two consecutive lines rhyme (i.e., a couplet) or alternating lines rhyme.
- ZYX: This is a rhyming form of poetry in which the first line starts with Z, the second line starts with Y, and so on all the way through A. It is an alphabetical reversal of the classic abecedarian form.
- Three-cubed through nine-cubed (i.e., seven new forms): Three-cubed is a rhyming poetic form that has three total stanzas of three lines each, and each line has three syllables, for a total of 27 syllables, or 3-cubed(= 27). Either successive (e.g., a couplet) or alternating lines must rhyme. A four-cubed poem has four stanzas of four lines each, every line having four syllables. Examples continue through the nine-cubed form.

3. Different Approaches to Writing Poetry. This how-to chapter takes the reader through several ways to write poetry and examples of each. Eight original example poems are included, as well as parts of poems by other poets. Technical points, such as meter, flow, beat/cadence, poetic and literary devices, using description-rich words, syllable counts, and so forth are discussed.

INTRODUCTION

4. Mixing it Up—a Variety of Poetry. These 43 poems, many of which follow classical rhyming patterns, span the range from such traditional forms of poetry as rhymes, limericks, and haikus (Japanese) to newer forms such as crystalline, etheree, and sausage poetry.

5. Around the World. Some of these 15 poems include styles of poetry from numerous cultures and continents, while others are about different areas of our planet.

6. Resources and Support. This is the final chapter, which lists and briefly describes a number of helpful references and online resources and sources of assistance, inspiration, and support.

Near the end is a Selected Glossary of over 100 poetry-related terms, an integral part of this book, followed by an Index of Titles and an Index of First Lines. A brief section, About the Frontispiece Photos, is next. A Bibliography concludes the book.

Good poetry should catch the reader's attention, but great poetry ought to be moving and memorable. It is my sincere hope that this collection is the latter.

Chapter 1

Inspirational, Nature, and/or Relationship Poetry

"In all things of nature there is something of the marvelous."
—ARISTOTLE

Poem	Primary poetry type*
You Can Do It!	rhyme
Dare to Dream!	carpe diem
You Are Worth It	rhyme
To Uplift, or Live Adrift?	rhyme
Tell Them Now	rhyme
ABC's of Appreciation	abecedarian
Building Connections	villanelle
Looking to Sea	quatrain
Sunrise!	pantoum
My Inner Voice—Supportive Choice	dramatic monologue
Stargazing Reflections	haiku

INSPIRATIONAL, NATURE, AND/OR RELATIONSHIP POETRY

Rhythm of the Rain	rhyme
Solitude in Academia	rhyme
Freedom	acrostic
Freedom in Flight	rhyme
Soaring Symbol of Strength	jueju
Patriotic Pursuits	dramatic monologue
Mother	rhyme
Father	rhyme
To Be with Her	sonnet
Beth	acrostic
Holly	acrostic
Grandma	rhyme
Family Farm	rhyme
Across States, Similar Fates	bio
Sunshine Café	rhyme
Silently Seeking Nature's Voice	rhyme (in tetrameter)
Connecting with Nature	haiku
Time	rhyme
Glaciers are Weeping	personification
Sometimes	cinquain
Framework of the Forest	rhyme
Giant Sequoia—King of All Trees!	rhyme
An Eagle Goes Fishing	sausage

* See the Selected Glossary, following Chapter 6, for definitions of each of these forms of poetry.

You Can Do It!

You can do it—I believe in you!
To your values and dreams, please stay true.
Work hard, earn it, do all things right.
A clear conscience helps you sleep at night.

You can do it—you have the right stuff;
Notably when the going gets rough.
Fight the good fight, and never give in.
In the long run and life, you will win.

Dare to Dream!

Dare to dream all things, mild to mighty,
Yielding to no artificial bounds!
You're the one who gives meaning to them.
Others claim how foolish it all sounds.

Life sometimes hangs heavy on your dreams,
Tarnishing bright ideas with "rust."
Keeping their flickering flames alive
Takes vision, courage, will, and self-trust.

Believe in lofty ideals, and
Don't be trapped in your life, day-to-day.
Steady work on your dreams makes them real
And will keep them from fading away.

You Are Worth It

Every day and in every way, you are worth it.
Don't let anyone ever tell you otherwise.
Human beings intrinsically have value.
Leverage it with the good we do with our lives.

Pursuing those things that matter and last, such as;
Family ties, friends, stewardship, and creations.
Respect for all, compassion, and civility;
A dose of humility in our relations.

Beauty fades, fame is fleeting, fortunes can be lost.
What then shall be the measure of what we have done?
Being honest, ethical, and true to ourselves
Treasures our people and planet in the long run.

To Uplift, or Live Adrift?

I ponder my existence beyond the breakers,
Navigating depth's perils past shallows of youth.
Will I rise with the tides and lift up those near me,
Or will I drift along unanchored by the truth?

Avoiding a solo Melville-penned fate, or wreck,
Depends on my "see man" skills and good attitudes.
Striving to be a vessel of encouragement,
As my life's journey marks increasing latitudes.

Experience stored as miles pass under my keel;
To have all the answers, I surely don't pretend.
With care and service among my mental cargo,
I am ready to help any mariner friend.

And so it is for all who sail upon life's seas,
Constant watch on the horizon, helm, and radar.
Make no ties, steer alone, try to stay on course; or
Give the hope and guidance of a familiar star.

Tell Them Now

If you appreciate others, tell them now,
While it still can add to their sense of self-worth.
To wait is a mistake many make because
No one knows how much time they have left on earth.

If you admire her kind generosity,
Or how he selflessly gives to those in need;
Letting them know sooner rather than later
Encourages them to do other good deeds.

Gratitude has positive ripple effects;
Expanding circles—lives we affirm and touch.
Avoid regrets about dearly departed
By telling them now they matter and how much.

ABC's of Appreciation

Appreciate others in ways that fit their needs.
Bestow proper gratitude, not a rude shout-out.
Congratulate them on their many good deeds.
Delight in guidance they gave to those in doubt.

Encourage the best in all those around you.
Follow up on the happiness they have sewn.
Give thanks to those who help folks by what they do.
Have gratefulness be that for which you are known.

Include in your list of friends those who are kind.
Just tell them, "Thanks!" in the few moments it takes.
Keep those who serve others always top of mind.
Let them know the big difference their work makes.

Mention clearly how they improved someone's life.
Notice the good things they do, which no one saw.
Owe, then pay them thanks for easing someone's strife.
Praise may prevent the proverbial 'last straw.'

Quality, sincere thanks is truly the key.
Repay your debts and strive to be a giver.
Salute those who from pitching in do not flee.
Thank people whose goodness flows like a river.

Inspirational, Nature, and/or Relationship Poetry

Understand even the selfless need support.
Value those who reject the 'me-first' fashion.
Welcome ones who to others provide comfort.
'**X**erox' thanks by copying their compassion.

Yearn to be ready now to answer the call.
Zero in on making Earth better for all.

Building Connections

Instead of fractures, let me build connections,
Respectful relationships, not battle lines;
Risking my safe, solitary protections.

If not agreement, at least shared directions;
Finding common ground, not planting hurtful mines.
Instead of fractures, let me build connections.

Working through and overcoming objections,
A win-win is there if we look for the signs;
Risking my safe, solitary protections.

Talking may help spur some needed corrections,
Shared meaning bridging gaps like fast-growing vines.
Instead of fractures, let me build connections.

Compromise requires from both sides reflections;
Craft a deal for which the pragmatist in me pines,
Risking my safe, solitary protections.

To solve problems, let us make good selections,
So, truth and fairness of answer clearly shines.
Instead of fractures, let me build connections,
Risking my safe, solitary protections.

Inspirational, Nature, and/or Relationship Poetry

Looking to Sea

I walk along the ocean shore
Seeking refuge from all my strife.
The wave-soaked sand serves as my floor.
Stars guide my reflections on life.

I cast my gaze to ocean's roar
In search of helpful solutions;
Like countless other souls before,
Wanting more than trite locutions.

Just then a vessel passes by,
Its lights merely a few dim specks.
Its dip below horizon nigh,
Concealing those who ply its decks.

The steady din of waves breaking
Washes my consciousness to sleep;
'Til seagull's squawk gets me waking
And pondering the ocean's deep.

Now back to my thirst for answers,
For enlightenment from the seas;
Distant waves break—tiny dancers,
Possibilities in its breeze.

Maybe that's the sum of it all;
The shore's a retreat from our fuss—
A harbor from life's random squall,
But the steering is up to us.

Sunrise!

Ah, sunrise! A great time to seize the day!
For generations, it has been that way.
Climax—horizon the beacon does ply,
To steady lightening of eastern sky.

For generations, it has been that way,
But to many, this event still holds sway;
To steady lightening of eastern sky.
Slice of cosmos touching earth makes us sigh.

But to many, this event still holds sway;
Time for love, laughter, wonder, work, and play.
Slice of cosmos touching earth makes us sigh,
The light of truth clearer when sun is nigh.

Time for love, laughter, wonder, work, and play;
To which lovers, others have much to say.
The light of truth clearer when sun is nigh;
Sunrise—another chance to live our "why?"

To which lovers, others have much to say;
Climax—horizon the beacon does ply.
Sunrise—another chance to live our "why?"
Ah, sunrise! A great time to seize the day!

Inspirational, Nature, and/or Relationship Poetry

My Inner Voice—Supportive Choice

In times of trouble, face of fear, and other stress,
I benefit from an inner conversation.
Self-talk to remind me when I'm under duress,
I'm well-equipped to handle self-preservation:

"Can I raise my will to meet this situation,
Just as I have had to so many times before?
Is anything so unique on this occasion,
Beyond the values, thoughts, skills I possess—and more?

It's creativity and imagination,
Helping me from overdrawing my well of will.
Using all these gifts keeps me on the destination,
But that is not enough; I need something else, still.

Something deeper—fortitude reserved in my soul;
My best, last defense against what might wipe me out.
Striving to meet each challenge, though they take their toll;
Inner voice encouraging me, easing my doubt."

INSPIRATIONAL, NATURE, AND/OR RELATIONSHIP POETRY

Stargazing Reflections

Stargazing, I sense
the enduring universe
and my mortal self.

Rhythm of the Rain

While lying in my bed, I leisurely listen
To the gentle rhythm of the rain on the roof.
As I notice raindrops on the windows glisten,
My eyelids hang heavy, I become more aloof.

Now safe and warm at the end of my day's hurries,
Therapeutic drizzle helps wash away my pain.
Like a caring, comforting friend soothes my worries,
I turn once again to the rhythm of the rain.

Inspirational, Nature, and/or Relationship Poetry

Solitude in Academia

Homer, Aristotle, Hobbes, Locke, Goethe, and Crane;
Chaucer, Shakespeare, Dickens, Tolstoy, Whitman, and Twain;
Whose imaginations and toils helped to unfold
Stories, philosophies, and lessons to be told.

The inquisitive student absorbed in his books,
Contemplating and learning while everyone looks
At him with judgmental glances, as if to say,
"Strange seeing him indoors, even on this fine day."

But to him, the weather is of little concern
While he is satisfying his deep thirst to learn.
Taken in by tales of peasants, lovers, and knights,
And those waxing on people's and government's rights.

Just then, he feels a chilly draft, but no matter,
As he tugs at his worn jacket collar's tatter.
Off in the distance, he hears children playing games,
But no match for his fables with fanciful names.

Lost in some fiction, he really can't help himself;
He thirstily reads his way across his bookshelf.
Hungry—but his knowledge appetite can outlast,
He ignores stomach growls as the lunch hour has passed.

The reader pores on in utter fascination,
As if in a trance, but not caused by libation.
Searching, grasping, he is mentally enraptured,
With meanings bold to subtle all being captured.

Inspirational, Nature, and/or Relationship Poetry

In deep translation of the scenes, plots, and faces
Scribed in earlier times and in other places.
He can wait for frolic, frills, and things of that kind.
For now, the scholar will sit and enrich his mind.

Freedom

Freedom is never free.
Respect our liberty.
Enjoy its many rights.
Expect it may cause fights.
Democracy survives,
Only if backed with lives.
May we not let it die.

Inspirational, Nature, and/or Relationship Poetry

Freedom in Flight

A graceful eagle soaring free;
Symbolizes our liberty.
Freedoms for which we paid a price;
In terms of human sacrifice.

Cannons, rifles, Revolution;
Bloodbath Civil War's solution.
'The Great War' didn't end all bloodshed;
On more battlefields soldiers tread.

UN action in Korea;
Containment was the idea.
Next the jungles of Vietnam;
Showed limitations of the Bomb.

Libya, Iraq, Afghanistan;
Still relevant is combat hand-to-hand.
Despite increased technology;
Conflict's in our biology?

Nation born on "new" continent;
Freedom the great experiment.
Seven articles, ten rights, too;
Framework for our Red, White, and Blue.

Not just Founders' resolution;
Begat our new Constitution.
Farmers, shopkeepers took up arms;
To keep liberty from all harms.

Inspirational, Nature, and/or Relationship Poetry

Soldiers, sailors, civilians, and more;
Also kept tyrants from our door.
The rule of law and not of men;
Safeguards rights of each citizen.

Mighty eagle can choose its way;
Strong wings, talons, a bird of prey.
Freedom, like eagles, can take flight;
From our grasp if we don't do right.

Each generation has a choice;
Honor freedom or lose its voice.
If we don't defend and cherish;
Oh, how quickly freedoms perish.

Soaring Symbol of Strength

Graceful eagle freely soars
Over the land, over shores.
Evoking independence;
Portraying magnificence.

Sign of strength, freedom, power;
O'er many birds does tower.
Symbol of the USA,
From nation's birth, through today.

Inspirational, Nature, and/or Relationship Poetry

Patriotic Pursuits

"Give me liberty or give me death!"
Patriot Patrick Henry exclaimed.
To give his country just one last breath,
Nathan Hale regretted, not complained.

U.S. Revolution spawned its brave,
Casting off chains of a foreign king.
Freedom and independence to save,
To these young rebels was everything.

And what might today's patriots say,
If in just such a situation?
Would they also rise above the fray,
Of similar threats to their nation?

"Centuries ago this continent,
To a new, free country did give birth.
Democracy the experiment,
A republic unequaled on earth.

Let those who seek to destroy our rights,
Recall our past, tremble to their core.
U.S. patriots shrink from no fights,
And will defend liberty once more."

Inspirational, Nature, and/or Relationship Poetry

Mother

An expectant glow and a radiant smile;
Anticipating the day, it's all worthwhile.

A gentle kick, then some uncomfortable nights;
Looking forward to the many sounds and sights.

The months go by until the passage of nine;
And then all of a sudden—this is the time!

The pains of labor cause temporary strife;
Soothed by the joy and miracle of new life.

A mother bonds with baby first to nourish;
Later lessons teach her child how to flourish.

A kind word here, lots of encouragement there;
Many are the ways a mother shows her care.

From helping hands to a much-needed embrace;
A gentle touch, a loving stroke of the face.

Readying children for being out on their own;
Hoping they reap the best of what has been sown.

Adults still look to "Mom" for help on their way;
Knowing their mother's behind them, come what may.

Supporting them always right through to the end;
Love different, deeper than that of a friend.

So then, as a grandmother, cycles repeat;
But her love and compassion never retreat.

Sharing warmth and wisdom with each new child;
Her temperament, perhaps, a bit more mild.

And so, the circle goes much like no other;
Dear is the kindness and love of a mother.

Father

Co-leader keeping a family strong;
Hopes, dreams, and goals he helps nurture along.
Wise guidance coupled with a firm handshake;
Sharing advice about which paths to take.

A dad is all of this and much more, too;
Helps son(s), daughter(s) find what they want to do.
From son's crib time to her walk down the aisle;
A father's presence is there all the while.

Whether shoulder rides or trying out sports;
A father takes on roles of many sorts.
A servant-leader living as he should;
He helps his family and neighborhood.

Through life skills he helps others self-direct;
Showing them love, honor, and self-respect.
Bringing out the best in those he reaches;
Through patience, love, and the things he teaches.

Inspirational, Nature, and/or Relationship Poetry

To Be with Her

I struggle nobly to describe my love.
Her voice! It calms my soul like peaceful dove.
Desire for her burns deep within my heart.
Her beauty shames a priceless work of art.

To be with her is much of my life's joy.
I feel for Greeks who saved Helen from Troy.
I think about what life was like before.
Glad I've no other lover to look for.

Do I compare my love to starry night?
The countless lights that strive to be so bright?
Her grace and elegance cause me to sigh.
I am a better man when she is nigh.

To pass the time away from her is pain,
But worth it all when I see her again.

Inspirational, Nature, and/or Relationship Poetry

Beth

Beautiful person who's second to none;
Eyes of blue filled with love, laughter, and fun.
Truly blessed, we watched you grow on your way;
Heaven sent joy that February day.

Inspirational, Nature, and/or Relationship Poetry

Holly

Holidays inspired the name we bestowed upon you;
Overjoyed to have you join our family of two.
Lovely, kind, and thoughtful, you continue to amaze;
Learning, growing, and maturing with the passing days.
You strive to define and reach your life's meanings and ways.

Grandma

With your sweet smile and thoughtful touch,
Care and kindness—you gave so much.
Mother, teacher, and farmer's wife—
Many the roles you played in life.

To me, you are Grandma always.
Life, love, and laughter filled our days.
Doing the chores, walking the land;
When trouble called, you held my hand.

A few tough times—we always fought 'em.
Your husband left us in the autumn.
When my father passed, you lost your son.
And we "did our darndest" to move on.

You graced us for 20 more years;
Lots more laughter, a trace of tears.
Guiding me from your place of peace;
Memories of you will never cease.

Family Farm

To my siblings and I while growing up,
The peak of summer was a fortnight each on the family farm.
In sharp contrast to cramped city living,
We loved the fresh air, open spaces, and all that country charm.

Grandma welcomed us with love and great food,
Such as garden produce, fresh eggs, and berries picked just that day.
Grandpa, while looking after fields and flock—
A man of few words showed affection for us in his own way.

Farm days began early, before first light,
With rooster's crow, livestock to tend, and machinery to run.
We looked forward to a hearty breakfast
Of warm eggs, toast, and bacon once the initial work was done.

After clearing dishes and daily chores,
We had a chance to spend some precious time with each grandparent.
Going for a hike in the fields or woods;
Helping Grandma make meals, watching Grandpa fix an implement.

There were farm rules we had to follow;
"Don't leave the hen house door open," and, "Don't play in a grain bin."
We also learned some "do's" of life, such as
Truth, the Golden Rule, and to love our family and all our kin.

Inspirational, Nature, and/or Relationship Poetry

We truly treasured each night on the farm,
Hearing crickets chirp and owls call as in settled the eve.
Clean skies let thousands of stars shine brightly.
With love sown and grown by our grandparents, we didn't want to leave.

Across States, Similar Fates

One man born in Schenectady, New York, before the Great Depression;
The other in Milwaukee, Wisconsin, before the moon-landing mission.
Two northern states that are geographically hundreds of miles apart,
But the values and lives of both men are not that different at heart.

Each dreamed big and pursued knowledge at prestigious universities;
Yale and Northwestern, respectively, providing opportunities.
One chose engineering, the other liberal arts and Navy tour;
Neither settled down yet as their futures had to unfold and mature.

Separated by three dozen years, yet each was restless and yearning;
Both enjoying family, friends, travel, hunting, and life-long learning.
With shared values of supporting local schools, teams, and love of this land;
Each a proud husband and father, respecting his wedding vow and band.

Working for a better community, economy, and country;
Holding ideals of truth, faith, freedom, enterprise, work, and liberty.
Thus, like many things in life, it goes in so many iterations;
Stories of friendship and similar fates between generations.

Sunshine Café

My daughter was growing up, becoming more independent;
One day we had a falling out, causing each of us to vent.
Saying unkind words and accusations we didn't really mean;
Both of us eventually storming away from the scene.

The next day I sat brooding while trying to do work at home;
When the idea hit like inspiration for a poem.
What if I were to harness the beautiful weather that day;
And transform my sunroom into a cozy sunshine café?

Quickly I tidied up and then made signs and decorations;
Short time before her return from school drove my preparations.
In the kitchen, I strived to cook my daughter's favorite fare;
Hoping to show her, "I'm sorry," and that I truly do care.

When she walked through the door, looked around, and saw all I had done;
Her countenance changed from anxiety to something more fun.
Together we talked, laughed, and dined at our little restaurant;
Healing the relationship with her had been my biggest want.

From this experience I kept a small Sunshine Café sign;
To keep and pull out sometimes when my daughter and I would dine.
Reminding us that between life's raindrops lies brighter weather;
And our Sunshine Café is near whenever we're together.

Inspirational, Nature, and/or Relationship Poetry

Silently Seeking Nature's Voice

In silence, I seek nature's voice,
Connecting me with other life.
To walk or hunt or fish—my choice;
I ease away from nagging strife.

If I would like a level field,
Without a road, or dam, or fence;
No bow or pole—no thing I wield,
Relying just on what I sense.

When I to nature most attune,
To birds and beasts and fish and more;
Is when I strive for peak commune,
Perceiving all that nature bore.

Inspirational, Nature, and/or Relationship Poetry

Connecting with Nature

Ditching high-tech toys,
I connect and commune with
Earth's natural scenes.

Time

Time, the great equalizer, yet mastered by none;
Deadline's enemy, said to fly when linked with fun.
An endless river flowing toward the future;
Excites planners anticipating adventure.

Asset? Liability? Depends on one's use;
To daydreamers, it can be a life-wasting muse.
Valuable to those who save early in life;
But wait too long, and it engenders later strife.

A claimed healer of wounds, helping many forget;
Prior mistakes, harms, other sources of regret.
Time moves steadily forward, present becomes past;
Outpacing people, places, things that do not last.

Inspirational, Nature, and/or Relationship Poetry

Glaciers are Weeping

For thousands of years, ice giants were sleeping.
But now, these dense "blue ice" glaciers are weeping.
Warnings that in many ways bear repeating.
Global climate change speeds glaciers' retreating.

In Alaska and Glacier National Park,
The melting of ancient glacial ice is stark.
Half the world's glaciers—in Land of Midnight Sun(1),
But in Glacier NP(2), soon there will be none.

Years hence, will Alaska have any at all?
Loss of these ice treasures, a clear wake-up call.
Value majestic Alaska, like Seward(3)?
Care for glaciers; each of us a good steward?

Alaska's Exit Glacier—leaving for good?
Will black stone stand where Blackstone Glacier once stood?
In Montana, Blackfoot Glacier shrinks each day.
The other twenty-five headed the same way.(4)

Glaciers' demise may get more than them crying.
Their loss may mean Earth's human life is dying.
Glacial and polar ice death no mystery;
If we do nothing, glaciers are history.

Signed,
Saddened for the Sobbing, Shrinking Glaciers

(1) Alaska is known as the Land of the Midnight Sun.
(2) National Park is often abbreviated "NP."

(3) Then U.S. Secretary of State, William H. Seward, negotiated the United States' purchase of Alaska from Russia in 1867.
(4) According to the U.S. National Park Service in 2018, "in 1850, there were an estimated 150 glaciers" in Glacier National Park. As of August 2018, there were only about 25, many of which are only remnants of what they had been.

Sometimes

Sometimes
Dark storms move in;
Strong winds, lightning, thunder.
Nature's rage spent, may bestow a
Rainbow.

Framework of the Forest

An oak stands its ground for many a decade;
Its acorns a squirrel's delight.
Versatile maple yields sap, hardwood, and shade;
Distinctive leaves trap the sun's light.

Ash and elm also help frame up the forest;
Weeping willow touches the stream.
And though some claim that its wood is the poorest;
Box elders seek a sunlight seam.

White or canoe birch with its paper-like bark;
Quickly captures woodworker's gaze.
Fir's snow-draped splendor in winter's day or dark;
Recalls warmth of past holidays.

Cedars resolute against wind and weather;
Resist moths and other such threats.
Mahogany girded with bark like leather;
Nice grain a craftsperson covets.

While further north right up to the timber line;
In the land of the evergreens.
Miles of aspen, cypress, spruce, and mountain pine;
Show just what "forest" really means.

Inspirational, Nature, and/or Relationship Poetry

Giant Sequoia—King of All Trees!

Giant Sequoia, king of all trees!
Standing mightily against the breeze.
Home in California USA;
Inspiring beholders to this day.

Growing more than 300 feet tall;
By living volume, reigns above all.
Some are over 3,000 years old;
Their wood resistant to fire and mold.

Yet, forest fires help maintain their ranks,
As does huddling near moist river banks.
Evergreen trees with lovely red wood;
US Parks protect them as they should.

The largest among them in terms of mass,
General Sherman, in its own class.
Waterfall Tree has the greatest girth,
And Reedwood is the tallest on earth.

No matter what the type of measure,
Each tree is a natural treasure.
Viewing their presence oh-so-stately;
Centuries ago or just lately.

Inspirational, Nature, and/or Relationship Poetry

An Eagle Goes Fishing

Eagle
eyes
salmon
near.

Raptor
reacts—
sharp-eyed
dive.

Eagle
ensnares
salmon
now,

With
his
strongest
talons.

Chapter 2

Brand New, Innovative Forms of Poetry

"Poetry can do a lot of things to people. I mean it can improve your imagination. It can take you to new places. It can give you this incredible form of verbal pleasure."

—BILLY COLLINS

Poem	Primary poetry type*
Serial poetry: three series—A, B, and C	
A. Spring, Summer, and Two More; Seasons Cycle through Four	
The Promise of Spring	serial (A—#1 in a series of 4)
Summer's Allure and Time to Mature	serial (A—#2 in a series of 4)
Autumn Harvest and Last Call of Fall	serial (A—#3 in a series of 4)
Winter Dormancy, Death, and Deliverance	serial (A—#4 in a series of 4)

Brand New, Innovative Forms of Poetry

B. Raining, Draining, Life-sustaining

Liquid Life	serial (B—#1 in a series of 3)
Skies Raining, Fields Draining	serial (B—#2 in a series of 3)
Rivers' Motions Refill Oceans	serial (B—#3 in a series of 3)

C. Five Phases of Our Lives

Childhood: Rising Up, Sizing Up	Serial (C—#1 in a series of 5)
Young Adulthood: Finding One's Path	Serial (C—#2 in a series of 5)
Early Middle Age: Calling, Career, and Clan	Serial (C—#3 in a series of 5)
Late Middle Age: Children Take Flight, a Second Light	Serial (C—#4 in a series of 5)
Elderly/Golden Age: Time for Shedding Some Tears, but Still Meaningful Years	Serial (C—#5 in a series of 5)
Books	acrostcrete
Fish	acrostcrete
Flag	acrostcrete
Decades of Distraction	deca
Deliverance at Dunkirk	deca
Friends for Different Ends	deca
Zest to Travel the 50 States of America	ZYX
Some Obscure Meanings Eclipsed; References Archaic, Research Enlightening; Meanings Attached to Them Each Relevant, Still (SOME RARE MATTERS)	ZYX
Ships and Boats from Z to A	ZYX

BRAND NEW, INNOVATIVE FORMS OF POETRY

Carnival	3-cubed
Games and Sports	3-cubed
Volunteers	3-cubed
Baseball—Good Call!	4-cubed
Leave it out There	4-cubed
Creative Desire	5-cubed
Willingness to Teach	5-cubed
Drive-in Movie Memories	6-cubed
The Allure of Lighthouses	7-cubed
Admiring Heavenly Bodies	8-cubed
Storms Around the World	9-cubed

* See the Selected Glossary, following Chapter 6, for definitions of each of these forms of poetry.

BRAND NEW, INNOVATIVE FORMS OF POETRY

I. SERIAL POETRY
A. SPRING, SUMMER, AND TWO MORE: SEASONS CYCLE THROUGH FOUR

The Promise of Spring

The promise of spring is a time of rebirth.
Plants rise from their slumber and re-green the earth.
Hibernators from their dens searching for food;
People sad from winter find a better mood.

Days getting longer, with more time to play;
Blue skies replacing those of white and gray.
Snow retreats to the highest mountaintops,
While farmers anticipate this year's crops.

The buds on the trees and the sprouts in the fields,
Hint at, but don't reveal their final yields.
Like an audience relishing a song just sung,
Animals give birth to and then nourish their young.

Trout in the streams and the robins return,
To build nests and feed their young do they yearn.
Refreshingly clean is the spring mountain air.
In meadows time passes with hardly a care.

Ball fields now echo the many seasons there spent;
The striping is fresh, the grass no longer dormant.
The sandlots alive with aspiring young players,
Chasing their dreams of making it to the majors.

Skyscrapers, roadwork, and other projects approved;
Progress from drawings and plans to dirt being moved.
Changing the skyline, landscape, and look of it all;
Energy, urgency—beat the deadline this fall!

The new season releases pent-up hopes and labor,
But gives us little time to pause, reflect, and savor.
That on this bridge to better days can we build;
The promise of spring is a promise fulfilled.

Summer's Allure and Time to Mature

Spring's promise transitions to summer solstice;
Plants striving to reach their full magnificence.
Young animals growing while herds roam the range;
Growth, maturity, and adapting to change.

Days now dominating the shortness of night;
The July sun burning especially bright.
People head to the pools and flock to the shore;
In retreat from the heat, yet still wanting more.

They seek recreation in valley and park;
Stories and campfires persist well after dark.
Students treat themselves to a late morning rise;
Brief escape from classes they'd have otherwise.

The mercury's rise leaves some bodies well-tanned;
But too much results in a parched, wilted land.
Humidity saps the will of the athlete;
Who digs down deeper to focus and compete.

Families travel on their long holiday;
Leaving favorite places but wanting to stay;
Streams and lakes yield surrounding's reflections;
And evoke unique summer recollections.

Lazy days growing up with not much worry;
Fun-filled days with friends flash by in a hurry.
Baseball games, beaches, grilling out in the yard;
Finding simple pleasures was not very hard.

Drive-ins and stargazing during cool August nights;
Late summer brings work and school back into sights.
Waning days stir summer memories in all;
Preparing for autumn and last call of fall.

Autumn Harvest and Last Call of Fall

Hot summer days yield to the cool autumn breeze;
A colorful display precedes falling leaves.
Colleges beckon students back to their halls;
Hunters practice goose, pheasant, and turkey calls.

The autumnal equinox, then harvest moon;
Coincides with the silence of the lake loon.
Piers are brought in, floats removed from their tether;
While cabins are readied for colder weather.

Crops soaking up the diminishing daylight;
Farmers strive to get autumn's harvest just right.
Reapers toiling afield to bring in the crop;
A lovely sunset provides a fleeting stop.

To days full of crisp, invigorating air;
Winter anticipating its looming share.
Ripe pumpkins both bountiful and versatile;
For Halloween, baking, or gracing a sill.

Now facing earlier dusks and later dawns;
Frost's icy fingers creep over roofs and lawns.
Indian summer serves as a warm encore;
The brief respite it gives leaves all wanting more.

Autumn is a time to take into account;
Another season's end—take stock as they mount.
Like leaves that pile up on now less fertile ground.
Hoping that meaning in life still may be found.

Brand New, Innovative Forms of Poetry

Thanksgiving helps bond families one and all;
Special time together before fall's last call.
Harvest's completion signals fall's final dance;
To winter dormancy, death, and deliverance.

Winter Dormancy, Death, and Deliverance

The year long in the tooth, the crops have been gathered;
Forests' autumn cloak lies mostly torn and tattered.
Cool fall evenings replaced by the late season gust;
Winter steals in as a cold betrayer of trust.

Slowly, yet steadily, the mercury recedes;
Dormant grass more fortunate than the dying reeds.
Geese leave the fields, heading south for another;
Water frozen like its terrestrial brother.

Then the snow descends upon us in a fury!
Sunlight not penetrating skies gray and dreary.
Wind-swept snow reshaped like dunes on a beach;
The warm allure of summer now seems far from reach.

Sub-zero cold arrives with its dangerous bite;
Giving pause to travelers, especially at night.
Sidewalks and drives shoveled, we seek shelter indoors;
Hot chocolate and marshmallows are winter's s'mores.

Month after month we tire of the polar vortex;
With sad folks, burst pipes, and winterkill, among its effects.
Deer and wildlife who couldn't escape its icy snare;
Lay where they fell, a caution to others who may dare.

Inside we hunker down while the sun is just a glint;
While outside signs of deliverance give us a hint.
Dripping icicles signal water starting to flow;
And remind us of the life buried beneath the snow.

Brand New, Innovative Forms of Poetry

Ice dropping from trees shows winter melting away;
Anglers and kids enjoy final days of ice play.
Winter's part of the cycle of everything;
Its waning days beckoning the promise of spring.

B. Raining, Draining, Life-sustaining

Liquid Life

Heavy, gray skies are weeping;
Into the ground it's seeping.
What doesn't run off remains;
Bountiful life it sustains.

Refilling rivers and streams;
An endless cycle it seems.
Evaporates to ascend;
Rains again and keeps the trend.

Skies Raining, Fields Draining

After gray skies rain, fields drain.
Saturation is streams' gain.
Ground seepage adds to the flow,
Running to where land is low.

Trickles collect, form a creek;
Larger waters it does seek.
Tributaries in motion—
Rivers flow to the ocean.

Rivers' Motions Refill Oceans

Volume helps rivers run fast;
Flood stages often surpassed.
Supporting life all the while,
Whether Amazon or Nile.

Rivers' motions like torrents;
Draining Great Lakes—St. Lawrence.
Sun's heat—ocean's top retreats;
Rain water cycle repeats.

C. Five Phases of Our Lives

Childhood: Rising Up, Sizing Up

During the time before children's memories last,
An infant's and then toddler's carefree days are passed.
Youngster keeps growing and learning along the way,
While parents hope values and good habits taught stay.

The "tween" years—bridge to changes and many a mood;
Testing ground for coolness a teen hopes to exude.
Friends, driving, "experiments"—peer pressure withstood;
Finishing high school starts the path of young adulthood.

Young Adulthood: Finding One's Path

At 18 comes tech school, military, college?
Apprenticeships, other ways to gain job knowledge.
Earning a living now but one major part;
Pairing and saving up—a family to start.

Trying new things—creative, hobbies, sightseeing;
To discover and unlock one's inner being.
Though life unfolds not always according to plan,
A worthy pursuit—one's calling, career, and clan.

Early Middle Age: Calling, Career, and Clan

At 36-plus, talent and treasure gained;
Calling and career may include family sustained.
Both clan leaders share roles and into them put heart;
To their offspring—love, values, and wisdom they impart.

Finally, their children pass through trials of youth;
Good citizens, lifelong learners, seekers of truth.
Hopeful they're ready for the world, children take flight.
Parents may have a renaissance—a second light.

Late Middle Age: Children Take Flight, a Second Light

Stealthy five decades-plus creep up—age 54;
Empty-nesters have a chance to seek meanings more.
Noble thoughts, missions, deeper realization;
Higher-level needs—self-actualization?

Rekindling, unshelving talents below the surface;
Developing or helping a greater purpose.
Loved ones' or thine own mortality may bring fears.
Time for shedding tears, but still meaningful years.

Elderly/Golden Age: Time for Shedding Some Tears, but Still Meaningful Years

Retirement generates both comfort and query;
A golden reward, perhaps, for bodies weary.
Delighting in grandchildren may be a given;
But toward what other ends might seniors be driven?

Passing of family members, friends yields sorrow;
Even so, elders can still welcome tomorrow.
Sharing experiences meriting veneration;
They help guide and raise up the next generation.

II. ACROSTCRETE POETRY

Books

Bi-covered treasure,
Offering much more;
Oodles of pleasure,
Knowledge in store;
Savor at leisure*

---

* The English pronunciation rhymes with "pleasure." [An alternative American pronunciation imparts a long "ē" to the first two vowels (ei).]

Fish

Freshwater or marine,
In plain sight or unseen;
Swim to angler's delight,
Have value in own right.

Flag

FOR A NATION, STATE, CITY, CAUSE OR OTHER;
LEADING SYMBOL THAT UNITES WHEN IT IS FLOWN.
ALLEGIANCE TO IT – LIKE SISTER OR BROTHER;
GARNERING RESPECT WHEREVER IT IS SHOWN.

III. Deca poetry

Decades of Distraction

Last 20 years—decades of distraction;
Americans "Idolize"* musicians.
While churchgoing is down—more inaction;
Voters don't learn about politicians.

We TV-show vote, not in elections;
Phones, streaming, social media nation.
Endless new technology selections,
Yet less personal communication.

We fight ourselves more, defend less our shore.
Focus: Civic virtue we must restore.

* A reference to the television show, "American Idol" (2002-2016, 2018-), in which viewers voted which musicians advanced to the next rounds, became finalists, and ultimately won each season's show.

Deliverance at Dunkirk

Late May to early June 1940;
Epic deliverance at Dunkirk, France.
Hundreds of thousands—their backs to the sea;
Fled to Britain through Nazi mistakes, chance.

Nazis seized Belgium early in the war,
Surrounding British, Belgian, and French troops.
Leave by English Channel—they couldn't do more.
800-plus boats, ships took them in groups.

300,000-plus Allied souls saved;
Four years hence, Allied victory flags waved.

Friends for Different Ends

Friends come in many types and times in life.
Some seek a being greater than mankind.
Others' best friend is their husband or wife.
Self-reliance alone a few do find.

Wise 20-plus-years' friend gave advice sage;
On friends of the road, and friends of the heart.
Former's shared journey done, they turn the page.
Latter you embrace after years apart.

My confidant is right, but in the end,
I still notice the loss of any friend.

BRAND NEW, INNOVATIVE FORMS OF POETRY

IV. ZYX POETRY

Zest to Travel the 50 States of America

Zest-filled to travel to all the states in our great nation;
Yearning for family to see more than one location.
Xenial aids like interstates, national parks, and more;
Washington through Wyoming—W states total four.

Virginia, Vermont—both boast forested mountains pretty;
Utah—industry, Rocky Mountains, and Salt Lake City.
Tennessee, the Volunteer State; Texas, the Lone Star State;
South Carolina—wrens; South Dakota—monuments great.

Rhode Island, the Ocean State, USA's smallest in size;
Querying online travel sites helped us avoid false tries.
Pennsylvania, the Keystone State, was a long drive across.
Ohio, Oklahoma, Oregon—gath'ring no moss.

New Hampshire to New Mexico—eight N states in total;
Maine coastline to Montana mountains—eight M states in all.
Louisiana, Pelican State, has the Big Easy.
Kansas wheat, Kentucky bluegrass—both thrive where it's breezy.

Journeying by car, plane, ferry, and train—but not rikshaw;
Idaho, Illinois, Indiana, and Iowa.
Hawaiian Islands were lovely but a long flight to reach;
Georgia—home to Atlanta, its capital, and the peach.

Florida—sandy beaches, swamps, gators, afternoon rain;
Enjoying learning much about our country is our gain.

BRAND NEW, INNOVATIVE FORMS OF POETRY

Delaware, the First State, has counties numbering just three;
California, Colorado, Connecticut—beauty.

But four A states helped enlighten us like a corona:
Alabama, Alaska, Arkansas, Arizona.

(As no doubt the reader has noticed along the way, both this poem and its title have gone from Z to A!)

Some Rare Matters

Some
Obscure
Meanings
Eclipsed;

References
Archaic,
Research
Enlightening;

Meanings
Attached
To
Them
Each
Relevant,
Still [SOME RARE MATTERS]

Zoetic, an adjective, pertains to life;
Yawl, a sailboat, cuts through water like a knife.
Xanthodont—having yellow teeth like rodent;
Wigwam, teepee—Native American tent.

Vant, an obscure form of vaunt—to boast about;
Ultimity—the last stage, the "final out."
Tele-words increase with more technology;
Stroma—organ's framework in biology.

Brand New, Innovative Forms of Poetry

Rejoinder is an answer to a reply;
Quicksilver—mercury—metal toxic, spry.
Pinchbeck—copper, zinc alloy imitates gold;
Obtend means to oppose, a term that is old.

Noetic—elating to the intellect;
Maladroit—one's moves have less skillful effect.
Lunarian is one who studies the moon;
Knub—husklike envelope of a silk cocoon.

Joinhand—an obscure term for cursive writing;
Insurrect is to rise up, as in fighting.
Hip roof has sloping ends and sides, no gable;
Gusset—metal can brace corner of table.

Flittermouse—a rarely used term for a bat;
Eft—a small lizard or newt; imagine that!
Dissite means separate, found apart;
Chico—a shrub found in U.S western part.

Bushel basket—a dry, eight-gallon measure;
Archaic words are rare, but still a treasure!

(As no doubt the reader has noticed along the way, the first word of each of the lines has gone from Z to A! Also, this poem has an acrostic title—Some Rare Matters.)

Ships and Boats from Z to A

Zille—flat-bottomed boat, may have a hut amidships;
Yacht—pleasure boat or ship, some can make ocean trips.
Xebecs have pronounced overhanging bow and stern;
Waka—canoe, to build the Maori did learn.

Viking ships—slender, with sails, oars, and a true keel;
Umiak—boat's wood frame covered by skin of seal.
Trawlers—for fishing, or naval use to mine sweep;
Submarines can be swift and silent, and run deep.

Roll-on/roll-off ships move many a container;
Q-ships—well-armed merchants on Navy retainer.
Paddle steamers' river use Twain often stated;
Ore ships—*Edmund Fitzgerald*, sometimes ill-fated.

Narrow boats work the thin canals of Great Britain;
Motorboats range from yachts to small boats you sit in.
Lifeboats have truly been a people-saving craft;
Ketch is a two-masted vessel rigged fore and aft.

Junk—ancient Chinese sailing ship still used today;
Inflatable boats—riders hope seals don't give way!
Houseboats can be as fancy as some homes on land;
Gondolas—Venice gondoliers propel by hand.

Ferries take people across seas, rivers, and lakes;
Escorts protect other ships, whatever it takes.
Dinghies—small boats carried or towed by one bigger;
Catamaran's twin hulls steady, like outrigger.

Brand New, Innovative Forms of Poetry

Barge, brig, battleship—their varieties are neat;
Argosy—a large merchant ship—one or a fleet.

(As no doubt the reader has noticed along the way, the first letter of each line has gone from Z to A!)

V. Three-cubed through Nine-cubed poetry

Carnival

Games, food, rides,
Lots of fun,
Giant slides!

Tilt-A-Whirl,
Dizzy-spun,
Boy or girl!

Coaster glides,
Day is done,
Happy strides!

Games and Sports

Games and sports
Can unite;
Many sorts*.

Sportsmanship,
Doing right,
Gamesmanship.

Fields, pools, courts,
Test your might**;
Games and sports.

* Games and sports can unite many different types of people and athletes, and games and sports each come in many sorts.
** Depending on the game or sport, this may include mental, emotional, physical, team, and/or other kinds of might.

Volunteers

Volunteers
Show they care,
Help their peers;

And others,
Being there
Like brothers.

Through the years,
Anywhere;
Volunteers.

BRAND NEW, INNOVATIVE FORMS OF POETRY

Baseball—Good Call!

When spring is here,
Baseball is near.
Nigh April 1,
Season's begun.

Opening day
'Cross USA.
From Young(1) to Spahn(2),
Pitchers were drawn.

The Babe(3) or Hank(4)
Home runs they'd crank.
Hits by Cobb(5), Mays(6)
Filled summer days.

Decades of games,
Other stars' names.
Legends in fall;
Baseball—good call!

(1) Denton True "Cy" Young, a right-handed pitcher who played for teams in the National League and American League between 1890 and 1911, won more games (511) than any other person in U.S. Major League history. U.S. Major League Baseball's top award for pitchers is named after him.
(2) Warren Edward Spahn, a left-handed pitcher who played for several teams in the National League between 1942 and 1965, won more games (363) than any other lefty in U.S. Major League history, despite missing three full seasons (1943-45) serving with distinction in the U.S. Army during World War II.
(3) A reference to George Herman "Babe" Ruth Jr., who hit 714 career home runs (HRs) between 1915 and 1935 while playing for teams in the National League and American League.

(4) Henry Louis "Hank" Aaron hit 755 round-trippers (HRs) between 1954 and 1976 while playing for teams in the National League and American League.
(5) Tyrus Raymond "Ty" Cobb accumulated at least 4,189 hits (second all-time in U.S. Major League history) playing in the American League from 1905 until 1928.
(6) Willie Howard Mays Jr. collected 3,283 hits playing in the National League from 1951 until 1973.

Leave it out There

First whistle sounds,
Will knows no bounds.
Leave it out there,
Nothing to spare.

To never yield,
Lay it on field.
But do not skip
Good sportsmanship.

Your heart and soul
Behind one goal.
Empty the shelf
For team and self.

End of the game,
Do not feel shame.
You went full stride,
Walk on with pride.

Creative Desire

A creative spark
Resides in us all.
A light in the dark,
A desire, a call,
A want—leave your mark.

Those who rely on
What inspires only;
To themselves a con
That leaves them lonely,
When the spark is gone.

Imagination
Needs true work and drive,
And cultivation
For it to arrive
At destination.

To paint, some do long;
The visual arts.
Play, sing, write a song,
Taps musicians' hearts;
Other ways not wrong.

Make things which appeal,
Not just on a lark.
Add practice to feel,
To harness that spark;
Make concepts real.

Willingness to Teach

Willingness to teach;
Others' minds to reach
Through examples, speech.
To share thoughts, I yearn;
Build desire to learn.

Imparting sage tips,
Some from my life's clips
Or gained from my trips;
Knowledge from living,
Mine for the giving.

Info they can use;
Classic themes and views,
Or more recent news.
Goal is they "get it"
And don't forget it.

Think chronology,
Weigh technology
And biology;
Help them acclimate.
Make sure they relate.

Learning is a flow,
Not just what you know.
But sharing it, so
Help them as speakers
And knowledge seekers.

Drive-in Movie Memories

I watched a cartoon movie
One night with the family
At the Starlite Outdoor.
But wait—there was still more!
Went to Kopp's for ice cream;
It all seemed like a dream.

Tagged along with brothers
To a bunch of others,
Like Victory Drive-in.
For fun, we were strivin'.
Highway 15 Outdoor;
41 Twin—screens four.

All changed in the '90s.
The edges of counties
Were being developed.
Drive-ins were enveloped.
Land sold and screens torn down.
Survivors in small town.

Milwaukee's eleven*
Soon dwindled to seven.
And by 2002,
All the drive-ins were through.
Last was 41 Twin
Located in Franklin.

Brand New, Innovative Forms of Poetry

We sure were lucky ducks;
Carload in for 10 bucks!
Brought snacks to feed our brood,
And snack bars served hot food.
Saw two movies—or three;
Used the playground for free.

We saw what was in store,
And patronized them more.
Keep this simple pleasure –
American treasure.
41—our kids knew
Before it bid adieu.

* This included the greater Milwaukee metropolitan area.

The Allure of Lighthouses

Lighthouse—sentinel seaside;
A welcome sight, steadfast light.
To mariners, a true guide;
Beacon helping them steer right
Whether in high or low tide.
Beam of light, helpful at night;
Gives sailors a safer ride.

Lighthouses help guard the coast,
Warn of fog, hazards, and more—
Reef or shoal cloaked like a ghost.
Small skyscrapers of the shore;
Michigan—state with the most
Lookout towers during war
Other Great Lakes states do host.

Michigan lighthouse—White Shoal;
Red, white stripes diagonal;
It looks like a barber pole;
Once had bell and fog signal.
Skillagalee—top like coal;
Its shape is octagonal;
Island home like an atoll.

Wisconsin—County of Door,
Cana Island Lighthouse sits.
Split Rock—Minnesota's shore;
Rests atop where the cliff splits.
Erie's Lorain Light no bore;
Caps two-story house with glitz.
Engineers built—Army Corps.

Brand New, Innovative Forms of Poetry

Coasts have lighthouses to see.
Statue of Liberty light
First used electricity.
Cape Hatteras is a sight.
At Hatteras Point, NC,
200-plus feet—most height.
Maine's Cape Neddick—three-story.

Point Reyes—"San Fran" CA.
Pigeon Point—in Golden State;
With white spire, active today.
North Head Lighthouse shares same fate;
Ilwaco, WA.
Eldred Rock built fairly late;
On namesake island—AK.

Lighthouses' inspiration
Shines with versatility,
Beyond just navigation—
Mix of style, locality,
Range, and illumination.
Standing with vitality,
And drawing fascination.

Admiring Heavenly Bodies

Sensing the amazing night sky
Always gets me pondering why.
Each part of our solar system;
Taking stock so I don't miss them.
Planets such as Venus and Mars
Appear larger than background stars.
With telescope, I more attune
To Jupiter's many a moon.

I note the absence of moon on Earth;
Its presence yields stargazing dearth.
Sometimes on a very clear night,
I spot a man-made satellite,
Or a comet or shooting star;
In relative terms, not that far.
I, by the zoom telescope brings,
See Saturn and its frozen rings.

Beyond sun, moon, and planets nine,
To take in more wonders, I pine.
To see stars in their locations;
Part of galactic formations.
Constellations—people did try
To find pictures in the night sky.
Like Orion the Hunter's bow,
Or Southern Cross in latitudes low.

Outer stars of Big Dipper's bowl,
Merak and Dubhe play a role;
Point to Polaris, the north star,

Brand New, Innovative Forms of Poetry

On Little Dipper's handle far.
Little Dipper—part of Small Bear;
Great Bear—Big Dipper is a share.
Cassiopeia's W,
Its five stars are easy to view.

Galaxies made of many stars,
Like the Milky Way, which is ours.
Million-plus galaxies to see,
Andromeda and LMC,
Whirlpool, Tadpole, more it is said,
Like NGC Thirteen Hundred [1300];
Cigar, Pinwheel, Sombrero, too;
More listed in Galaxy Zoo.

Individual stars appear
Though from us many a light-year.
Sirius, with "Dog Star" nickname,
Brightest star in sky is its fame.
Alpha Centauri—three stars tight,
In night sky is the third most bright.
Red supergiant Betelgeuse,
Celestial star version of Zeus?

Other heavenly bodies' roles,
Include nebula clouds, black holes.
Though white dwarf stars are near their end,
Heat energy they still expend.
Much unknown about universe;
Big Bang's energy does disperse?
Novas, pulsars, neutron stars, and more;
There's still a lot left to explore.

Brand New, Innovative Forms of Poetry

For as long as man's been around,
He has gazed upward from the ground.
To behold that beyond his home,
Pushed by innate desire to roam?
Traveling space for 60 years,
In man's thoughts, and at times, his fears.
On each clear night, some stop and stare,
To learn more about what's out there.

Storms Around the World

By many names—storms around the world;
Which hemisphere, nation's flag unfurled?
In West, coasts hammered by hurricane,
Storm surge, heavy rain, wind speeds insane.
Hurricane's eye provides brief reprieve,
But storm's backside seems to never leave.
Named storms—Katrina, Sandy, Andrew;
Death and damage tell us they passed through.
To heal and rebuild took years to do.

Aussies call it a willy willy.
To some, such a name may sound silly.
To the west and east, they are cyclones.
Further north, a typhoon; Neptune moans.
In Caribbean, they're called tempests,
With all the worries that name suggests.
All of which shows—no matter what the name,
Nature's power and rage still the same;
Reminds all of where and when they came.

With less force, tornadoes still a threat;
Those who love them don't soon forget,
Their swirling winds, suction, freight train sound;
How heavy objects were tossed around.
Twister—an alias for this storm;
Resulting debris field still the norm.
Vortex at sea is a waterspout,
But of their danger, there is no doubt.
Wise captains steer an alternate route.

Brand New, Innovative Forms of Poetry

Thunderstorms bring rain, lightning, thunder;
At times, hail tearing things asunder.
In Asia, monsoons saturate land;
Coastal regions' large waves soak the sand.
Landslides, mudslides a constant danger;
On low ground, flooding is no stranger.
Straight-line winds can be part of the mix.
More dangers when energy upticks;
T-storms can spawn nasty weather tricks.

Eskimos have 50 words for snow.
Whiteouts are storms wherever they go.
Snowfall and sleet make road travel tough;
Snarl airports with too much of the stuff.
Slowing trains as snow piles up on rails;
Main winner may be snowmobile trails.
True blizzards* are not much of a treat.
Ice storms can down power lines with sleet,
Leaving people without lights and heat.

Other events can wreak havoc, too;
Haboobs—dust storms—hard to see, drive through.
Dust Bowl harmed many in U.S. West;
Killed some; put others' will to the test.
Heat waves also claim many a life;
Parching droughts cause cattle and crops strife;
Drying up streams, creeks, rivers, and lakes.
Survive doing whatever it takes;
Cracked ground, roads part of what the sun bakes.

Brand New, Innovative Forms of Poetry

Earthquakes a storm somewhat turned around,
Globe's tectonic plates' moves shake the ground.
From tidal waves with 90-foot highs,
Or more, tsunamis make boats capsize.
On land, build volcanoes' lofty heights;
When inactive, adorn landscape's sights.
Suddenly, their cones can turn aglow,
Spew ash, lava around and below;
When it will erupt is hard to know.

A new storm may pose the most danger;
Global warming could be a game-changer.
Polar caps' melting makes oceans rise.
Glacial ice loss adds to problem's size,
Higher oceans flood cities on shore;
Now-extreme storms become even more.
Positive feedback compounds the trend;
'Til nothing we do can make it end.
Too-warm atmosphere we cannot mend?

How can we avoid a world too hot?
Insects, disease, infrastructure shot?
Technology warns us in advance,
Of storms' approach, giving us more chance,
To change plans, take shelter, or else flee,
From a hurricane or tsunami.
But science can't be our sole tether,
Binding us to solve world-changed weather.
To save Earth, we must work together.

* This is also a trade name of an ice cream dessert at a popular U.S. fast-food restaurant chain.

Chapter 3

Different Approaches to Writing Poetry

"I would define, in brief, the poetry of words as the rhythmical creation of Beauty."
—EDGAR ALLAN POE

"Carry a big basket. In other words, be open to new ideas, different partners, and new practices, and have a willingness to dump out the old and irrelevant to make room for new approaches."
—FRANCES HESSELBEIN

The unexamined life is not worth living."
—SOCRATES

As I mentioned in the Introduction, good poetry should catch the reader's attention, but great poetry ought to be moving and memorable.

Different Approaches to Writing Poetry

Accessible

I also believe poetry should be accessible to readers and writers. This means that, even if it takes some effort (e.g., re-reading, sometimes deciphering the bard's poetic license, etc.), the poem is fairly understandable to the reader. It also means that the poem's words "pay for themselves" (i.e., are justified in their inclusion). A poem which conveys significant meaning in a succinct way helps make that poem more memorable, powerful, and efficient.

Poetry does not have to rhyme (e.g., blank verse, free verse, etc.), but if it strays too far from identification as a meaningful collection of words that conveys a definite theme or themes using a recognizable flow, meter, rhythm, and/or pattern, it is no longer poetry but something else (e.g., an essay, narrative, letter, manifesto, etc.). All that stated, much can be learned from the unconventional styles and approaches of such late American poets as Emily Dickinson (1830-1886) and Langston Hughes (1901-1967), as well as more "contemporary" (post-World War II) poets around the world.

Inspiration and work

In terms of subject matter and themes for my poetry, as noted in Chapter 1, one source is inspiration. Many things inspire me, such as truth, love, family, freedom, people doing the right thing, worthy causes, a greater good beyond ourselves, hope, beauty, friends, nature, learning, the joy of discovery, helping others, innovation, teaching someone something and they "get it," people striving to be their best, creativity, the universe, stargazing, particularly memorable moments or times in others' lives as well as my own, and so much more. For instance, my travels have inspired me to write poetry. I wrote 10 poems during a trip to Alaska, and I wrote other poems during a trip to Hawaii. However, you don't have to travel thousands of miles for inspiration. Inspiration can be as close as specific interactions and relationships with family members and friends, carefully exploring your own backyard, or simply enjoying the beauty, peace, and serenity of a local park, river, lake, field, woods, glade, mountain, valley, etc.

However, I do not rely on inspiration alone in writing poetry, nor do I labor uninspired for hours plying my craft. Rather, it is a combination of both, plus other motivations such as a genuine interest in conveying an important message, the meaning, use, origin, truth, effect(s), beauty, feeling(s), etc., of words, and more that drive me in this form of expression. I truly enjoy reading and writing poetry. It is at once a creative, learning, reflective, and communicative experience. One of my main goals of this book is to help make it easier and more enjoyable for you to read and write poetry, too.

Forms of poetry

I wrote and included in this collection approximately five dozen recognized forms of poetry, and I created 11 new forms of my own (please see Chapter 2). I enjoyed challenging myself to write forms of poetry with which I was previously less familiar. I researched and studied hundreds of existing forms of poetry and stretched my poetry writing to include many of them. Details about many forms of poetry are included in the Selected Glossary near the end of the book. All of that said, I have a slight preference for more traditional, rhyming poetry. In fact, when writing poetry, usually my default approach is to think in rhymes.

Literary/poetic devices and elements

Once you have selected the form of poetry you wish to use and topic(s) about which to write, you also need to think about the mechanics of actually writing your poem. One such consideration is the *meter* of your poem. Meter refers to a recognizable pattern of stressed and unstressed syllables. Stressed, or emphasized, syllables are the hard—or long—component of a word, and unstressed syllables are the soft or shorter portions. Meter helps provide a rhythm to the poem, which is particularly apparent when the poem is read aloud. Poems in English can utilize five different types of meter, but the one I focus on here is the iambic meter. An iamb is a metrical foot comprised of an unstressed (or short) syllable followed by a stressed (or long) syllable, like so—da DUM.

Two of the more commonly used forms of iambic meter are tetrameter (i.e., four meters—da DUM da DUM da DUM, da DUM) and iambic pentameter (i.e., five meters—da DUM da DUM da DUM da DUM da DUM). Slight or occasional departures from either pattern are allowed, such as one extra or missing syllable. The late English actor, playwright, and poet, William Shakespeare (1564-1616), was a master of iambic pentameter, using this metrical form in over 150 sonnets, each of which was typically 14 lines long.

Very similar to meter, the overall cadence of a poem can be used to promote a consistent "beat" or "pulse" of the poem, or the length and/or pace of successive lines can be varied to emphasize certain key feelings, characters, events, etc., or to build to a climax (e.g., the late American poet, Edgar Allan Poe [1809-1849], did this effectively in such poems as "The Bells"). This is done through choice of the number of syllables per line, the specific arrangement and sequence of words (i.e., how you say it) including alternative wording (e.g., the character Yoda from the original "Star Wars" film series was very clever at this), using descriptively rich words, including obscure and/or archaic words, and so forth. The use of such literary devices as alliteration, analogies and similes, metaphors, irony, humor, and sarcasm keeps your poetry interesting.

Incorporating imagery that captivates the reader and, through the pictorial sense such imagery conveys, develops shared meaning and a deeper connection with the reader. The ancient epic poet, Homer, wove compelling imagery into his two best-known masterpieces, *The Iliad* and *The Odyssey*. Where appropriate, using such poetic devices as internal rhyme, parallelism, play on words, and other techniques furthers that connection and makes the poetry more moving and memorable. Remember, not to overdo it, though. Each literary/poetic device used should advance your

DIFFERENT APPROACHES TO WRITING POETRY

poem in some way. Too often, I have seen a poem's lesson lost in the literary/poetic devices used, especially with excessive internal rhyme. Do not let the mechanics of the words get in the way of the poem's meaning and message. I have long been impressed with the economical use of words—yet effectiveness of the writing—by the late authors Ernest Hemingway (1899-1961) and Isaac Asimov (1920-1992), as well as current author, Janet Asimov (a.k.a. J. O. Jeppson).

Creating a title for each poem

A thoughtful title for each poem is very important. Think of it as the headline for your poem, because it is. A well-written title is summative (i.e., concisely tells what your poem is about), meaningful, and memorable. Consider each poem for which you can recall its title, and my guess is that a particularly relevant, catchy, and/or short title helped you remember each of them. A poem's title can incorporate one or more of the literary/poetic devices and/or elements discussed above. A particularly good title can almost be a poem by itself. Some examples of this are "Dare to Dream!" (page 4), "To Uplift, or Live Adrift?" (page 6), "My Inner Voice—Supportive Choice" (page 13), "Stargazing Reflections" (page 14), "Rhythm of the Rain" (page 15), "Freedom" (page 18), "Freedom in Flight" (page 19) "Soaring Symbol of Strength" (page 21), "Across States, Similar Fates" (page 32), "Time" (page 36), "Glaciers are Weeping" (page 37), "Baseball—Good Call!" (page 78), "Subtle Call of Waterfall" (page 133), and "A Wonder Down Under" (page 169), among others.

A good title can also subtly convey and connect two related concepts, providing even more meaning. For instance, consider "Looking to Sea" on page 11. Yes, one must look towards the sea to observe the far-off waves breaking, the ship passing by, etc., but one must also be *looking to see* anything! Please do not underestimate the importance of an effective title. An inspiring title can motivate people to read the rest of your poem, especially if it is relatively short and, therefore, a quick read for them. I know this because people have told me so. For instance, based to a large extent on getting them interested with my title, people have gone on to read "You Can Do It!" (p. 3), "You Are Worth It" (p. 5), and "Tell Them Now" (p. 7). If you can also deliver a truly inspiring poem to go with that title, now you really have something!

Examples of writing poetry

Having discussed a basic background of poetry and some characteristics and elements that make it a unique and attractive form of literature, it is time to walk through some examples of writing original poetry.

- An acrostic is a form of poetry in which typically, although not always, the first word of each line spells out one word (or more) that is (are) often the title of the poem but does not have to be. A good example is the poem, "Elizabeth," by Edgar Allan Poe. The first letter of each line of Poe's poem spells out, "ElizabethRebecca." Now, let's say your name is Sarah. Here is a simple example of an acrostic poem I wrote using that name:

Sarah

Sincere in caring about her peers;
Assuring them all despite their tears.
Relationship rich beyond her years;
Agile enough to quickly change gears;
Her friendship elicits many cheers.

Notice that the last word of each line rhymes (this is not required for acrostic poems), making this acrostic also a monorhyme.

What if the subject's name is Stan? Here is another basic example of an acrostic I wrote using the name, Stan:

Different Approaches to Writing Poetry

Stan

Second
To
Almost
None

Obviously, I have a pretty high opinion of both Sarah and Stan! This "Stan" acrostic is called a vertical monocrostic, since it is a vertically-oriented acrostic with one word in each line.

For more examples, please see my other acrostic poems, "Freedom," "Beth," and "Holly," on pages 18, 27, and 28, respectively.

- Another simple form of poetry is one in which the even-numbered lines rhyme. One such poem I can recite by heart from my childhood (i.e., it is memorable) is, "An Emerald is as Green as Grass," by the late English poet, Christina Georgina Rossetti (1830-1894). Two examples of my poems that are structured this way are "To Uplift, or Live Adrift?" (page 6) and "Tell Them Now" (page 7). For an example in which the first and third lines, and the second and fourth lines, of each four-line stanza rhyme, please see my poem, "Patriotic Pursuits," on page 22.

- Here is another basic form of poetry in which every other line rhymes (and notice the effort at internal rhyme within the first line—"full" is a near rhyme with "dull"):

Ready for the Road

Car running well, its tank full; he slept much, so mind not dull.
Though GPS* was working, he had a backup phone "app."**
Travel plans shared with friends, and alert against mental lull,
He felt ready for the road and almost any mishap.

Different Approaches to Writing Poetry

* GPS is short for global positioning system, which commonly refers to a GPS receiver/device which detects geolocation and time information anywhere on Earth where there is an unobstructed line of sight to four or more global navigation system satellites which transmit this location and time data. Some obstacles (e.g., buildings, hills, mountains, caves, tunnels, etc.) may block GPS signals.

** App is short for application, one of thousands of typically downloadable computer programs which provide specialized information.

An example of a longer poem which follows this format is "Looking to Sea" on page 11. Adventure poetry is one of my favorite areas since I literally get to tell a poetic story about one or more of my adventures. Some examples of this are "Zest to Travel the 50 States of America" (p. 69), "Supersonic!" (p. 120), "Community Creek" (p. 123), "Sudden Storm" (p. 124), "Root Beer River" (p. 126), "Camping Trip" (p. 128), "Road Trips" (p. 130), and "Recreational Retreat" (p. 160).

- Another poetic form, the rhyming couplet, consists of two rhyming lines, as in the following brief example:

Fair Thrills

Somewhere among this fair's iron hills,
I'll find a coaster that gives me thrills.

For additional examples of poems that use rhyming couplets, please see my poem, "Mother" (which consists of 13 rhyming couplets), on page 23, as well as the last two lines of my Shakespearian sonnet, "To be with Her," on page 26. For examples of poems in which two consecutive lines rhyme in each of their four-line stanzas, please see my poems, "Freedom in Flight" (p. 19) and "Soaring Symbol of Strength" (p. 21).

- In the abecedarian form of poetry, the first line starts with the letter A, the second line begins with B, and so on through the twenty-sixth line which begins with Z. A modified version, the ABC form, follows this same pattern but can be less than 26 lines long, as in the following example:

A Form of Poetry that Uses ABC

An abecedarian poem—one should not forget,
Begins each line with the next letter of the alphabet.
Continuing that pattern throughout the rest of the piece,
Delivering a form the bard can use through Z, then cease!

- For a longer example of an ABC form, please see my poem, "A Birthday Card," on page 122.

- For an abecedarian example, see "ABC's of Appreciation" on page 8.

- A simple two-line poem, in which each two-syllable line rhymes, is called a footle. Footles usually deal with lighter topics in an amusing, witty, ironic, or sarcastic way. Here are two very elementary examples:

Rhyme Time

Made rhyme
> In time

Lighten Up

Uptight
> Made light

- Another simple example is "Final Footle" on page 162. Extending this concept, a footle series consists of multiple footles within the same poem. Please see my examples, "Gaining Ground" (p. 116) and "Elusive Poet" (p. 117). To me, writing good footles and footle series is simultaneously fun, challenging, and rewarding.

- Another form of poem, the simple Etheree, was named after the late Etheree Taylor Armstrong (1918-1994) of Arkansas, who invented it. A simple Etheree is a 10-line poem in which the first line has one syllable, the second line has two syllables, and so on through the 10-syllable tenth line. The lines do not have to rhyme, but they can. There should be an identifiable, overall message or theme to the poem. An Etheree has 55 syllables in total, as shown in the following example:

DIFFERENT APPROACHES TO WRITING POETRY

Poem Could Be an Etheree

This
Poem
Could just be
An Etheree,
And be more worthwhile,
While following that style,
And show that it does belong.
Form's founder—Etheree Armstrong,
With 55 syllables to pen,
Increased by one each line's from one to ten.

- For two examples of the Etheree form of poetry, please see "Fear" (p. 146) and "Free—Basic to First Amendment" (p. 156).

Summary

In summary, reading and writing quality poetry is more accessible today than ever before. As detailed in Chapter 6, there are numerous printed, online, and other resources available to assist, encourage, and support aspiring poets. Writing good poetry takes some work, but it should also be a fun, creative, expressive, and reflective process. There are literally hundreds of forms of poetry from around the world, and new forms are being created each year. I highly encourage you to explore all of them before settling on your favorites.

Numerous literary/poetic devices exist that you can use to enhance your poems and make them more significant, moving, memorable, and powerful. We walked through how to write several simple examples of different forms of poetry to enable you to

Different Approaches to Writing Poetry

get started right away on your poet's journey. Additional examples of each form and many more are included throughout this book, and various literary/poetic devices are employed, too. Part of the fun is learning how poets use such devices in different and creative ways to connect with their readers while still making the key points of their poems.

Remember that penning a body of quality poetry is a marathon, not a sprint. You should enjoy the journey and the scenery along the way. Like many things in life, you are likely to get out of writing poetry what you put into it. Please consider your audience, too, as that should also help inform your writing. I highly recommend that once you have written a rough draft of a poem, you take the extra time and care to spell and grammar check it, verify the rhyme scheme and syllable counts, reflect on what you have written, review it, refine and revise it (if necessary), and revisit it again. I have often revised a poem years later in an effort to make it better.

Choosing the right structure for your poem is important, too. For instance, a haiku is used to juxtapose two ideas or images, with a switching or cutting word in between them to cue the reader as to how the two concepts are related. As such, a haiku can be an opportunity to quickly and impactfully compare and contrast, and therein lies its beauty. If you want to expand upon your ideas, images, stories, experiences, or whatever is the subject of your poem, consider a longer form such as a Rispetto (eight lines with a rhyme scheme of a-b-a-b-a-b-c-c; see my example, "Recreational Retreat," on page 160), sonnet (14 lines in total length, often divided into three quatrains each with a conventional rhyme scheme, followed by one concluding rhyming couplet), or narrative poetry, which provides plenty of lines and space for the author to more fully develop the details of his/her poem.

Well-written poetry can be beautiful, inspiring/moving, powerful, and/or impactful, and when truly done right, all of those things simultaneously. Consider, for example, the many leaders (e.g., U.S. President John F. Kennedy in 1963, numerous university presidents, and high school speakers at commencement addresses through the years, etc.) who have quoted the last three lines of

DIFFERENT APPROACHES TO WRITING POETRY

Robert Frost's poem, "The Road Not Taken" (from his 1916 book, *Mountain Interval*) which are:

> Two roads diverged in a wood, and I—
> I took the one less traveled by,
> And that has made all the difference.

That shows the power and impact of great poetry, which is both moving and memorable. On a much smaller and personal level, I happened to read my poem, "Mother," to my mom within the last three years of her life. I could tell (plus she told me) that she was genuinely touched. I read it at her burial, and the family members present were also moved. To me, all of this reaffirms the beauty, inspiration, power, and lasting significance of quality poetry. Quality prose and poetry endures—from excellent work produced by ancient philosophers (e.g., see *Ideas of the Great Philosophers* by William S. & Mabel L. Sahakian, 1966) and poets (e.g., Homer's *The Iliad* and *The Odyssey*), as well as Renaissance and Enlightenment-era ones (e.g., see, for instance, *The Complete Works of William Shakespeare* (1997, Wordworth) and *The Age of Reason* (1951, Cornell University Press), respectively) to top-notch publications by some of today's authors.

Use your imagination and be creative. Do not be afraid to experiment. Push the edges and the envelope itself—a lot. Try writing many different forms of poetry on a wide variety of topics, as did the late American poet, Robert Frost (1874-1963), and the late Japanese haiku master, Matsuo Bashō (1644-1694). Over time, you will develop distinctive elements of your own approach and style. For example, I write poetry about many different topics. One hallmark of my poetry is that I try to always leave the reader with something positive. Even with difficult or tragic topics, I try to at least provide a glimmer of hope. The ending of your poem is the last impression you leave with your reader, so finish well and make it count. Put your best efforts out there. Above all, have fun with it. For example, I enjoy writing humorous poetry, not only because laughing is a great way to relieve stress, but also because it gives me a break from more serious matters. If you want a smile right

Different Approaches to Writing Poetry

now, please read the first eight poems of Chapter 4, starting with "Seasick" on page 109. Having fun is the main thing that will keep bringing you back to poetry. I truly wish you good luck as you endeavor to become a bard. The poetic possibilities are practically endless!

Chapter 4

Mixing it up—a Variety of Poetry

"The poetry of the earth is never dead."
—JOHN KEATS

Poem	Primary poetry type*
Seasick	limerick
A Taxing Experience	light poetry
Up and Down, Round and Round	rhyme
Temporary Space, Personal Place	rhyme
What am I?	rhyme
Roll to Play	rhyme
Gaining Ground	footle
Elusive Poet	footle
A Hot Date	sausage
An Eyebrow-Raising Key to Electricity	clerihew
Supersonic!	rhyme
A Birthday Card	ABC
Community Creek	rhyme
Sudden Storm	rhyme

Mixing it up—A Variety of Poetry

Root Beer River	rhyme
Camping Trip	rhyme
Road Trips	Fibonacci
Stars' Sharing	concrete
Tree	concrete
Subtle Call of Waterfall	crystalline
Farms	lanterne
Maritime Missions	narrative
'Sailing' in Space to a Lunar Landing	narrative
Ignoring a Warning Left a Nation in Mourning	narrative
Titanic Tragedy	narrative
POW's Paradox	haiku
Lament from the Living	elegy
Fear	Etheree
Still a Brave New World Ahead: Cloning, Eugenics Not Dead?	rhyme
Some Simple Joys	rhyme
The Chill of Autumn, the Warmth of Romance	sonnet
Holistic	Pleiades
Innovation	Pleiades
Willpower	Pleiades
Inquisitiveness	diamante
Careful Concerning Contracts	tail-rhyme
Free: Basic to First Amendment	Etheree
Where Have Good Manners Gone?	satirical poetry
Could Have Rhymed but Doesn't	blank verse
Some of Life's Phases: In a Few Phrases	ninette
Recreational Retreat	rispetto
Canadian Geese: Still Roam or Stay Home?	choka
Final Footle	footle

* See the Selected Glossary, following Chapter 6, for definitions of each of these forms of poetry.

Seasick

A young man shipped out on the sea;
No care if 'twas windward or lee.
      But storms came along,
      His stomach not strong,
Now sees ships only on TV!

A Taxing Experience

A miser by any measure,
Who rarely had a word to say;
Until clerk of the town's treasure
Paid skinflint a visit one day.

"To what do I owe your presence?"
 It taxed the cheapskate to utter.
"Do not look to me for presents!"
The tax man screamed in a sputter.

"You now need to pay your fair share,"
Revenue man said at no length.
"Oh—as for sharing, I don't care,"
Miser replied, spending his strength.

"Pay, or I'll seize your cash and such!"
 Agent warned, to which miser said,
"My best assets you cannot touch;
I'll be frugal until I'm dead!"

Tax collector trying to stay cool,
Then asked, "Perhaps you'd like the cell?"
Miser responded, "I'm no fool;
With no frills, I've nothing to sell."

Frustrated to the point of tears,
But covering up with a shout.
"We'll get what you owe in arrears!"
The thwarted agent headed out.

His face turning to smile from frown,
Scheming to beat tax court duress;
The miser sold his place, skipped town,
And left no forwarding address.

Up and Down, Round and Round

You can walk the dog with me,
But you do not need a leash.
To go 'round the world with me,
You should keep me within reach.

Kids may like being with me,
But there is a string attached.
For ease of recalling me,
My sing-song name is unmatched.

My life has its ups and downs,
That's what I need to unwind.
If you wonder what I am,
A yo-yo is what you'll find.

Temporary Space, Personal Place

Providing a safe, steady place
For my toddler watching a play.
At times, a refuge for my pet
With me on a different day.

Then a perch for my computer,
Which lets me work 'most anywhere.
A handy place for my popcorn,
Viewing movies without a care.

So, if you really want to know
What I've been writing about here.
Please do not ask me to stand up,
Or else my lap will disappear!

Mixing it up—a Variety of Poetry

What am I?

I may have eyes, but I have no ability to see.
There are well over 5,000 varieties of me.

South America is where I originated from.
Another name for me is Solanum Tuberosum.

At least initially, my favorite place is the ground.
I can come in many shapes, but a side of me is round.

Like much of the world, you might just find me on your table.
With all these clues, identify me if you are able.

Roll to Play

Roll me, and with luck, you just might win;
Some people pay to try it again.
Others cheat by trying to 'enhance;'
The weight of my sides for games of chance.

If I'm in a board or "table" game;
My possible outcomes are the same.
I might matter more than my small size;
My lowest value is called "snake eyes."

Before you find trouble for yourself,
Recall I can range from two to twelve.
If you don't know by now, please think twice;
And you'll find that I'm a pair of dice.

Gaining Ground

Ran fast
    Still last

Felt down
    All frown

Time off
    Didn't scoff

Got rest
    More zest

Ate right
    Grew light

More drive
    To thrive

Worked out
    No doubt

Then ran
    Again

This time
    Sublime

Was first
    Not worst!

MIXING IT UP—A VARIETY OF POETRY

Elusive Poet

No rhyme
    This time

Re-thought
    Still naught

Read books
    Got looks

Brain nap
    A sap?

More rest
    Flunked test

Online
    Not fine

Didn't learn
    Still yearn

Free verse
    Got worse

Poet?
    Forget

Tried hard
    No bard!

A Hot Date

Excited—
Date!
Eager
Romance.

Enjoyed
Dinner,
Red-hot
Tango!

An Eyebrow-raising Key to Electricity

Benjamin Franklin, to prove lightning held electricity,
Flew a kite in a storm; attached to the kite cord was a key.
Though some thought this dangerous experiment was a bit odd,
Franklin sparked more inquiries and invented the lightning rod.

Supersonic!

Dawn had come, the sun was out;
And everything was just right.
Southern 'Cal' sky calling me;
For my supersonic flight!

The sleek F-14 Tomcat;
Tuned and ready for the task.
For what more of a true thrill;
Could a 19-year-old ask?

Into the pilot's skilled hands;
I completely placed my fate.
Lieutenant flying the aircraft;
And I his eager first mate.

Finding another Tomcat;
Simulating a dogfight.
Both of us doing our best;
To keep "bogey" in our sight.

We flew straight up in the air;
Both pulling multiple G's.
Clear canopy let us sense;
The wind speed but not the breeze.

Later, we both disengaged;
Flying level for a while.
Above the blue Pacific;
Around San Clemente Isle.

We fired the afterburners;
Swept back the wings to go fast.
Now flying supersonic;
Oh, how I wished it would last!

The main thing I noticed was;
Clouds going by more quickly.
Not wanting this flight to end;
Though it had made me sickly.

We practiced a 'touch and go;'
Before landing once again.
I thanked the pilot for this;
A peak in my life 'til then.

A Birthday Card

A birthday card when I was but a kid,
Brought something more than just the names it hid.
Caught between its two pieces of cardboard,
Dollars(!)—or a check—to help me afford
Elusive gifts I couldn't otherwise buy,
For fear that I would have to explain why.
Going to stores stretched my birthday some more,
Hoping whatever I bought, I'd adore!

Community Creek

Years ago, when my friends and I were just boys;
A nearby place provided such simple joys.
To us, it was one of the best local 'finds';
"Let's go to the creek," never far from our minds.

We usually rode bikes, although sometimes we'd run;
To be first to arrive was part of the fun.
Visiting each favorite spot with made-up names;
Racing leaf and twig boats, playing other games.

Covering stones with mud, shouting "Bombs away!"
Vying for biggest 'explosion' of the day.
Pretending that large rocks were islands mid-stream;
For hours, we'd play in a quasi-daydream.

Imagining that millimeters were miles;
Jumping from the creek's banks to 'fly' to warm isles.
When dusk called us home as it did way too fast;
We knew today's trip here would not be our last.

Sudden Storm

Visiting Grandma one hot and humid summer day;
My brother and I started out on a mile-long stroll.
To the lake and some shopping at the Country Boy store;
When all of a sudden in did the thunderclouds roll.

Only a quarter-mile more, "Can we make it?" we asked;
After lightning began striking with thunderous might.
"Press onward or turn back?" our looks said to each other;
By then the afternoon was turning as dark as night.

The storm-driven winds now made us brace our forward gait;
Raindrops pricking our skin like a thousand tiny spears.
Yards away, sparks flew from a power pole transformer;
Each of us trying different ways to soothe our fears.

I burst out in prayer for our safe deliverance.
While my brother just seemed to kind of go with the flow.
Neither of us choosing the optimal solution;
Not knowing whether to hunker down or try to go.

Deciding to head back to Grandma's safe apartment;
We ran as fast as we could while still ducking the lightning.
Our shoes sloshing through the country highway's soaked shoulder;
Warm thoughts of Grandma help block worries more frightening.

Through the torrent we see what appear to be headlights;
The car barely staying on the narrow asphalt strip.
At first passing us, then skidding sideways to a stop;
While we wonder who would make such a treacherous trip?

From the driver's window comes a familiar voice;
Our Uncle Stan is telling us to get in the car.
Hearing our transformer story, he calmly assures;
Tires insulate the car, and we don't have to drive far.

At Grandma's, we thank her and Uncle Stan for their help;
We learn that lightning struck that power pole on our route.
After the storm, my brother and I both realize;
We'll be a bit wiser before next venturing out.

Root Beer River

Looking forward to a relaxing weekend afternoon,
My son and I board and ease the canoe into the stream.
Happily do we paddle and guide our small, streamlined craft,
Our boat gently gliding through the depths as if in a dream.

The canoe gently slipping through the tea-colored river,
Tannin, lignin, peat, and humus each help color this moat.
While water-exposed tree roots collect whitish foam fungus,
Colors and textures combine to suggest a root beer float.

Onward we paddle, now increasing our effort and speed,
Arm and core muscles work in harmony with the current.
Our canoe lurches forward with every successive stroke.
So caught up in our journey, we wonder where the time went.

Even with hushed voices, we don't quite blend in with the scene.
Fish and waterborne bugs scatter, and a crane takes to flight.
Animals on the banks depart as silence eludes us;
Running out of time to finish our voyage before night.

Striving for stillness to not spoil picturesque beauty,
We cease almost all activity, the better to hear,
Nature's sweet symphony of wildlife and flowing water.
Quieting down more, we dip a paddle only to steer.

This oneness with our environment now having been earned,
Such a measure of tranquility not often achieved.
An approaching car stirs us as we float under a bridge,
And of our duty to solitude we sit now relieved.

Mixing it up — a Variety of Poetry

We approach our landing with a mix of feelings and thoughts.
Family bonds and shared experience form quite a tether.
The canoe stowed, we reflect on the day as we head home.
We'll cherish and miss our time on the river together.

Camping Trip

The car's loaded up with tents, sleeping bags, and the rest of our gear;
Looking forward to camping—can't believe it's been another year.
Trying to enjoy the drive with rest and relaxation in mind;
Anticipating fun times while hoping we left nothing behind!

Finally, we arrive, time to pick out our specific campsite;
Hurrying to pitch the tent and find campfire wood before night.
Those base tasks behind us, we unpack food, matches, and other goods.
Most of us set out to explore nature with a hike in the woods.

To those tending camp befall the supper-making duties and chores;
Heat the water, start the beans, get out all the materials for s'mores.
A hot meal awaits those returning from their forest commune.
We reflect for a moment on our good fellowship and fortune.

Then after we've dined and cleaned up, comes perhaps the best part of all;
We sit around the campfire and share stories and tales often tall.
After stargazing a bit, we fight sleep for the fire's last ember.
Bonds formed by these experiences are what we'll long remember.

Finally, we yield to heavy eyes after dousing the fire,
And we retreat to our tents, cots, and sleeping bags to retire.
As we begin to drift off, we become aware of the nighttime's refrain;
Chirping crickets, a hoot owl, and in the distance—a sandhill crane.

After what seems a blink, we awaken with dawn as the trigger,
To the cool and fresh morning air, imparting to us its vigor.
We unzip our tents and stumble out, hoping no one is looking,
And scurry about to light the fire and get breakfast cooking.

Today, we'll hike, canoe, fish, and take a dip in some nearby lakes.
As the day wears on and energy ebbs, we'll take some kind of breaks.
Thankful for several more days ahead in this camping lifestyle,
And the simple escape it provides from our hectic pace for a while.

Road Trips

I
like
road trips.
They teach me
about our country,
its cultures, and geography.
What's more, they're good for eliciting from me fresh quips,
such as the day my family took a car, bus, train, and plane, and even took a hike!

Stars' Sharing

As they clearly twinkle through midnight sky, I gaze up at the stars and wonder why. The universe shares its bounty with me. What did I do to deserve such beauty?

Tree

A treetop's leafy crown;

New growth an arborist sometimes trims.

Main branches stable but still growing;

From the tree's sturdier, mature limbs.

Tapers to protective trunk—

Solid core,

Conduit,

& much more.

Moisture-seeking roots

Spread like their above-ground counterpart—

Feeding the tree with nutrients, too—

Subsoil partner of tree's upperpart.

Subtle Call of Waterfall

Voluminous rush of waterfall—
Cool, soothing spray its subtle call.

Farms

Farms
Crops grow,
Livestock raised,
help sustain us;
fields.

Maritime Missions

Maritime missions—real and varying;
Connected by all being seafaring.
Whether gathering food or defending the shore;
Moving people and cargo, doing research, and more.

Planning the voyage, all aboard, load provisions;
Following the wake of centuries-old traditions.
Cast off all lines, clear shallow water, and chart the course;
Harkening back to Phoenicians and men of the Norse.

Sailing the high seas, steering the vessel, taking fixes;
First guided by stars, then sextants, and now electronics.
Stand the watch smartly, often check navigation;
Use radar and sonar, mind lookouts on station.

Hopeful always for fair winds and following seas;
Sunny days, starry nights, a peaceful ocean breeze.
Gently rolling ship, mariners drift off to sleep;
One of the simple pleasures of life on the deep.

But what's that ahead just over the horizon?
Storm clouds, rough seas, sailors best be arisin'!
Batten the hatches and stow all loose gear!
Trust the captain finds a safe course to steer.

No relief for now, the storm is getting worse;
Keep sailing and just endure Poseidon's curse.
Truly the windward and not the lee;
Ship and crew in peril on the sea?

Mixing it up — A Variety of Poetry

Finally, "It's dawn!" shouts the forward lookout;
The sea still raging and now a waterspout!
Quick—alter the course, hard to port!
 Steer around it—don't fall short.

Danger averted, continuing on track;
Relieved sailors welcome return to the rack.
Those still on watch breathe a sigh of relief;
Days of routine with occasional grief.

Swab the decks, work the galley, it's almost the dinner hour;
Below decks, the engine crew strives to keep the ship in power.
Look over there, starboard side, just past the rail;
Flying fish, racing dolphins, and a humpback whale!

Such can be the sights and sounds of the sea;
Crossing oceans, experiencing plenty.
Container ships with their roll-on, roll-off crates;
Other merchant vessels with similar fates.

USNS hospital ships named Comfort and Mercy;
Bring care and healing to people in many a country.
Research boats exploring undersea creatures;
Oceanographers updating charts' many features.

Naval vessels showing military might;
Protecting the homeland both day and night.
To aggressors no quarter, and pirates get the message;
For terrorists who would harm—there will be no safe passage.

Diverse purposes and tasks but united by wind and waves;
Of his ship and travels are memories a mariner saves.
Warning of rocks and reefs, the familiar lighthouse is beckoning;
With other aids to navigation, outdating dead reckoning.

Spotting near-shore buoys—red, right, returning;
The ship approaches port, engines still churning.
At harbor's mouth a tugboat waits;
Helping the vessel in with its many shipmates.

Now station the special sea and anchor detail;
Avoid hazarding the ship—at this, do not fail.
Eternal vigilance is never off the clock;
Until the vessel is tied safely to the dock.

'Sailing' in Space to a Lunar Landing

In 1492, Columbus set sail on the seas;
Nina, Pinta, Santa Maria driven by the breeze.
Backed by King Ferdinand and Queen Isabella of Spain;
Water route west to Asian spices was to be their gain.

But 30 years would pass 'til Magellan and/or his crew;
Crossed three oceans, then back to Spain in 1522.
Captain died before earth circumnavigation complete;
Wooden ships and cloth sails were more than equal to this feat.

Fast forward 400-plus years to 1969;
When the Cold War and the Space Race were now both top of mind.
US and Russia competing to have their flags unfurled;
First upon the familiar but far-off lunar New World.

President Kennedy's goal, about which much was written;
Land a man on the moon, and bring him safely home again.
The Mercury and Gemini programs helped pave the way;
For Apollo 11's moon landing that July day.

Left Kennedy Space Center by Saturn V rocket's roar;
Lifted off into space instead of sailing from the shore.
Moon trip took four days, helped from Houston by Mission Control;
Three men this time, not ships, each one playing a vital role.

Command Module *Columbia* evoked seagoing forebear;
Lunar Module *Eagle* flying last leg of lunar dare.
On the lunar descent, Aldrin and Armstrong proved quite deft;
Touching down with just 25 seconds of fuel left.

Armstrong said, "The *Eagle* has landed," on July 20.
Back in Houston, relief and celebration aplenty.
The next day, once the lunar surface Armstrong's boot did find;
"That's one small step for a man, one giant leap for mankind."

Parents telling kids, "Watch this history in the making!"
TV scenes and *Life* magazine photos both breathtaking.
Aldrin also walked the moon, then per the one-day schedule;
Eagle ascended to join Collins and Command Module.

Flight back to earth, Pacific splashdown July 24;
Three new moon minerals discovered and a whole lot more.
The moon shot shed light on this world community affair;
While barely illuminating how much more is out there.

MIXING IT UP—A VARIETY OF POETRY

Ignoring a Warning
Left a Nation in Mourning

Five years into the U.S. program of space shuttle flight,
On a cold Florida morning, very little went right.
The date—January 28th, 1986,
Challenger had the latest space shuttle avionics.

'Twas two years newer than *Columbia*, its sister ship,
Between the two spacecraft, it would be their twenty-fifth trip.
Its mission: do experiments and launch a satellite,
But ignored data and overconfidence sealed her plight.

O-rings sealing sections of solid rocket booster's hull,
The chance of them "seating" at 36 degrees was null.
Booster's rubber O-rings in cold temperatures turned hard,
Heeding statistics, delaying launch would have been safeguard.

Flight delayed six days due to weather, tech issues, and more,
Prompted NASA to launch cold—they had been lucky before.
At 11:39, *Challenger* took off and roared!
With seven people, including the first teacher, aboard.

During her brief, historic 73-second ride,
High speed, craft movement, and smoke concealed the wound in her side.
Hot gases escaping from the rocket booster's structure,
Heated the cold external fuel tank, causing its rupture.

Mixing it up—A Variety of Poetry

Not 10 miles above and east of Kennedy Space Center,
Challenger's explosion caused its pieces to re-enter.
But its solid rocket boosters kept flying for a while,
And the crew compartment ascended almost three more miles.

Finally free-falling into the Atlantic Ocean,
Challenger ripped by aerodynamic forces, motion.
Search recovered the crew compartment from the ocean floor,
Other parts of the orbiter, boosters, payload, and more.

President Reagan addressed a grieving nation that night,
Of service to country, the astronauts never lost sight.
Though *Challenger's* tenth and last flight never made it to space,
Its crew "slipped" earth's "surly bonds" to touch its Maker's face.

Fallen but not forgotten are Commander Dick Scobee,
Pilot Michael Smith, Mission Specialists numbering three:
Judy Resnik, Ellison Onizuka, Ron McNair;
Greg Jarvis, Christa McAuliffe—Payload Specialists pair.

New Hampshire's McAuliffe was to be the first teacher in space.
(Backup, Barb Morgan, later rode *Endeavour* in her place.)
Rogers Commission helped ground shuttles for nearly three years,
Until *Discovery's* '88 flight allayed some fears.

For 15 more years—not another shuttle tragedy,
'Til *Columbia* broke up on reentry in '03.
The catastrophe again took the lives of all seven.
And *Atlantis* flew the last shuttle flight in '11.

Titanic Tragedy

A dozen years into twentieth century;
A Belfast-born vessel became the world's envy.
Titanic carried immigrants with hopes and dreams;
Middle-class folks, famous people, and those of means.

From gyms and pools to grand staircase on this liner;
In terms of size and luxury, none was finer.
Her waterline measured almost 900 feet;
Titanic was the largest of White Star Line's fleet.

With coal-fired steam engines, she sported four smokestacks;
Decks 'uncluttered' with lifeboats let strollers relax.
'Watertight bulkheads' promised to make people board;
But as partial walls, ship's safety they didn't afford.

Of her voyages, this was *Titanic's* maiden;
With passengers, crew, and cargo was she laden.
Leaving Queenstown, UK, on a New York bound cruise;
Captain Smith in charge of *Titanic's* triple screws.

Full speed ahead! Good press for early arrival.
But too fast in an ice field risked her survival.
Ignoring ice warnings on her destination;
Tragedy targeted *Titanic's* location.

Lookouts with no binoculars helped seal her fate;
Crow's nest, "Iceberg! Right ahead!" warning came too late.
Her undersized rudder not letting her steer clear;
Ice caused substandard, hand-driven rivets to sheer.

Opening six compartments' hull plates to the sea;
Too many to keep watertight integrity.
Bulkheads could have stopped progressive flooding, but no;
Seawater spilled over them—they were built too low.

Most hoping to flee found a sad, similar plight;
Not a third of her souls boarded lifeboats that night.
Californian, within just 20 miles or less;
Ignored *Titanic's* rockets and calls of distress.

That left *Carpathia*, fully three hours away;
Even at her top speed, she could not save the day.
Hypothermia took those the lifeboats couldn't save;
1500 people to a watery grave.

For 73 years submerged in ocean deep;
'Til Ballard awakened her secrets from their sleep.
Iceberg did not rip a gash in *Titanic's* hull;
Nor was her side shattered due to brittle metal.

Iceberg's glancing blow caused iron rivets to pop;
Flooding two more compartments than bulkheads could stop.
Though she broke up, her stern didn't rise high in the air;
Her front section split off due to water's weight there.

From this disaster came improvements overdue;
Such as lifeboat space for all passengers and crew.
Better forecasts, ice warnings, ship design, safety;
To help reduce mariners' peril on the sea.

POW's Paradox

Prisoner of war [POW]
ponders the vast universe
in solitary*.

* short for solitary confinement, in which a POW is isolated from other inmates, often in cramped and dark conditions

Lament from the Living

My unknown older brother, I often think of you.
What would you have been like—your dreams, goals, and what you do?

The father I knew passed before our childhood was done,
What bonds you might have made with your granddaughters and son!

Grandpa, you were a man of few words, but even so,
Those happy times on the farm matter more than you'll know.

Grandma, your life was blessed with the longest hourglass,
Thanks so much for guiding me long after you did pass.

Fear

Fear,
To some,
A chance to
Show character,
While to others, a
Huge adrenaline rush;
Heart pounding, muscles tensing,
To confront the danger head-on.
Opportunity or enemy?
Not truly known 'til we face that moment.

Still a Brave New World Ahead— Cloning, Eugenics Not Dead?

Is government control of humans' birth, aging, and dying
In century 26, as practiced by a new World State;
Different from 20th century's use of eugenics,
Which used "fitness" to determine people's reproductive fate?

A high-tech London, where humans' material needs are met,
Setting of Aldous Huxley's, *Brave New World*, utopian tale;
Sterile world of human cloning and conditioning to castes,
Recreational soma drug and sex use on widespread scale.

In respite from his boss'—the DHC's—awkward confessions,
Bernard and Lenina fly to the Savage Reservation.
There they meet Linda and her young adult son, John "the Savage,"
Fathered by DHC 20 years before, on vacation.

Bernard publicly presents Linda and John to DHC,
Bringing Director of Hatcheries and Conditioning [DHC] down.
DHC flees from "sin" of involvement in natural birth.
Bernard and new celebrity, John "the Savage," gain renown.

Finally, John rejects the soma, sex, and clones of London,
Spurns Lenina's moves and keeps soma from "lower" Delta caste.
His retreat to do penance draws crowds and curiosity;
Leads to suicide by hanging—John's perceived freedom at last.

This Brave New World's parallels to eugenics cannot be lost,
Since, in both cases, the state had a hand in who lives and dies.
American Breeder's Association, "better babies,"
Forced sterilizations—how U.S. eugenics took its guise.

Human cloning now—gene, reproductive, or therapeutic—
Raises a host of ethical, moral, and other issues.
Somatic nuclear transfer to clone human embryos
Evokes Brave New World's 'soma' in copying people's tissues.

Eugenics—legal in U.S. until 1970's,
Its dehumanizing nature gone from society's norms?
With current human cloning research, genetic 'shopping,' more,
No one's safe 'til humankind is respected in all its forms.

Some Simple Joys

A run on the trail, a walk in the park;
Ending the work day, enjoying the dark.
A weekend with family, a night with friends;
Hard work in advance helps bring happy ends.

A scrumptious supper, a luscious dessert;
Texting the kids, taking in a concert.
A post-dinner drink, a joy in its sips.
Vast information at our fingertips.

A movie enjoyed, a snack to converse;
Being social, begging not to disperse.
For what other simple joys do we yearn?
Some shared here, but the rest we must discern.

MIXING IT UP—A VARIETY OF POETRY

The Chill of Autumn, the Warmth of Romance

Not really looking for romance that fall,
Instead intent to focus on my work;
And studying to find my real call,
I chanced upon her serving as a clerk.

Just getting to know her was quite a thrill—
A fine brunette with sapphire eyes ablaze!
As summer days gave way to autumn chill,
Her wit and charm continued to amaze.

To call on her was the highlight of my day,
No matter if we talked or walked or dined.
The way she brightened up fall's shades of gray
Convinced me of the value of my find.

When all was done, I'm glad I took a chance,
For love and marriage came from that romance!

Holistic

Holistic—complete view:
Health—spirit, body, mind.
High-tech—connects us through.
Happy—joyful mankind.
Hemispheres—Earth has two.
Hope—desires intertwined.
Human—global, not few.

Innovation

Inspiration, need, or both;
Idea born, attains growth.
Intuition, data drive,
If concept is to survive,
Ingenuity is key.
Iterations aplenty,
In model's move to market.

Willpower

Willpower, or self-control,
What's to be said of its role,
When many a researcher
Wrangle—nature or nurture?
Whole lot more study required—
Why some less mentally tired,
When stressors in life are fired.

Inquisitiveness

Inquisitiveness,
Plus education—
Including learned concepts,
Applied skills, experience—and
Life lessons, all
Lead to
Empowerment.

Careful Concerning Contracts

Read each contract, though you might squint.
Understand all terms and fine print.
Shield yourself in the deal.

If you even suspect foul play,
It may be best to walk away,
And don't affix your seal!

Free—Basic to First Amendment

Free—
Concept
Basic to
Constitution.
Its First Amendment
Keeps religion from state
Establishment and protects
Its free exercise and rights to
Speech, press, peaceable assembly, and
Petition the government for redress.

Where Have Good Manners Gone?

Oh, my! Where have good manners gone these days,
While impoliteness rudely overstays?

Presents received but thank-you's never sent;
No indulgence request before some vent.

Pushing past others with no, "Excuse me."
But when credit is sought, they say, "Choose me!"

A hasty departure with no goodbyes;
A crowded funeral where no one cries.

Golden Rule had tempered vulgarity;
Now Rule broken with regularity.

On our streets and highways, it's called road rage.
Driving out kind patience of prior age?

Some "leaders" don't deter hostility,
But instead "lead" in incivility.

New communication technology,
Yet we've lost power of apology.

Could Have Rhymed but Doesn't

Example here of blank verse poetry;
It uses iambic pentameter.
An extra syllable to close line three, so
This blank verse poem could have rhymed but doesn't.

Some of Life's Phases—In a Few Phrases*

Birth
Then growth
Listen, learn
Explore and do
Reach your destiny
Maintain plateau
Legacy
At peace
Death

* This Ninette is a sketch of some of life's unofficial phases in a few phrases (nine lines; 25 total syllables).

Recreational Retreat

When troubles and turmoil lay their grip on me,
Solace is found in a simpler time and place.
In my mind or person, it is where I flee;
Recalling Grandpa's tractor and Grandma's face.
Across spring-fed brook, past a massive oak tree;
Tall pines encircle and hide my hilltop space.
Nature soothes and recreates me to my core.
Friends' strife fades here, too; I've saved spots for more.

Canadian Geese: Still Roam or Stay Home?

Migratory birds
North American natives
Mate for life, protect goslings
White cheeks and "chinstrap"
Black head and neck, brown body
Fly in V-shaped formations
Making honking sounds
Go on migrating
Or settle in man-changed lands?

Final Footle

Reached end;
   Bard-tend!

Chapter 5

Around the World

"Being different gives the world color."
—NELSAN ELLIS

Poem	Primary poetry type*
Arctic Sustenance	rhyme
Antarctica—Cold, High, and Dry	enclosed rhyme
Northern Necessities	haiku [a Japanese form of poetry]
Aesthetic Africa	ghazal [Persian/Arabic/Urdu/Hindi]
A Wonder Down Under	rondeau [a French form]
The Southern Tier of Western Hemisphere	ottava rima [Italian/Sicilian/English]
Less Costs More at the Store	chastushka [a Russian form]
One Ancient Wall Stands Above All	jueju [a Chinese form]
Cosmic Context	questionku
Living Gratefully	tanka [a Japanese form]

Around the World

Terrestrial Travels	Than-Bauk [a Burmese form]
Sleek, Smart and Social Swimmers	jueju [a Chinese form]
Taught through Trails	kimo [an Israeli form]
New Approaches	monoku [a Japanese form]
"Rubbernecks" in Action, Cause Us More Distraction	senryu [a Japanese form]

* See the Selected Glossary, following Chapter 6, for definitions of each of these forms of poetry.

Arctic Sustenance

Paddling a kayak, rivers and great sea call;
To fishing waters and spacious hunting grounds.
Lines and harpoons the best fishing tools of all;
Hunt caribou making migratory rounds.

Summer brings Inuit umiaks to sea;
Seeking whale blubber to feed many a clan.
Seal hunting, ice fishing during minus degrees;
Sustain natives of pretty, challenging land.

Antarctica—Cold, High, and Dry

Last continent to which humans did divert;
Antarctica has highest elevation.
Frozen tundra limits its vegetation;
With slight precipitation—a cold desert.

Final Earth region sighted—1820;
98 percent covered by mile-thick ice.
Compared to Australia, its size nigh twice;
Subglacial lakes give it water aplenty.

Antarctic Treaty signed by 50 nations;
Protects ecozone of this land south polar.
During high summer, full days of light solar,
For thousands of people at research stations.

Despite harsh conditions, wildlife survives here.
Snow petrel, other birds have Antarctic home.
Fur seals, emperor penguins, other breeds roam;
One thousand-plus species of fungi appear.

Though it's the fifth largest continent in size,
Antarctica leads in average wind speeds.
Controlling sea levels, serving other needs;
Keeping Antarctic ice shelves stable is wise.

Northern Necessities

Sea—giver of food;
Ice—shelter's material;
Caribou—clothing.

Aesthetic Africa

Africa—Serengeti—its vast plains;
Lake Victoria—Nile River fast drains.

Kilimanjaro its loftiest mount;
Three volcanic cones and Kibo's mast reigns.

Continent hosts buffalos and monkeys;
Elephants, giraffes, gazelles find past lanes.

Clockwise migrate zebra, wildebeest, more;
Other beasts on which a lion fast gains.

Blessed with diamonds, cobalt, iron, and gold;
Having moved these goods to far coasts, passed trains.

Africa shows beauty in ways not few;
With its freshness, story is like last rains.

A Wonder Down Under

Land of gum trees, circled by seas;
With respect, we call them Aussies.
Remote middle is the outback,
Hardy peoples embrace its track;
There dwell some Aborigines.

Kangaroos, sheep—feel the west breeze.
Magpies warble up in the trees.
Dingos, wombats—there is no lack;
Land of gum trees.

Cultural centers also please;
Sydney, Melbourne, Brisbane—cities.
At bushwalking, some take a crack.
Natives often want to go back.
Land of gum trees.

AROUND THE WORLD

The Southern Tier of Western Hemisphere

A land of much diverse biology;
In South America, a dozen nations.
Rain forest helps the Earth's ecology.
Here Incas, others built civilizations.
The Andes Mountains—top geology;
Tobacco, cotton, cocoa grace plantations,
And mighty Amazon flows east of here.
The southern tier of Western Hemisphere.

Less Costs More at the Store

Shopper said to corner vendor,
"Time was, I could count on full bags."
Vendor told him, "Find a lender;
I am late for marking up tags!"

Around the World

One Ancient Wall Stands Above All

A human feat among all,
Lies in China—its Great Wall.
To keep Mongols, others out,
Shield China, prevent a route.

Over 13 thousand miles,
Surviving many trials;
Done in 206 BC.
Building it was not easy.

Cosmic Context

Trillions of stars;
Earth's human beings;
How do we all fit in?

Living Gratefully

We can decide to . . .
Respect others and ourselves,
Value our planet,

Be grateful for all we have,
Do the right thing every time.

Around the World

Terrestrial Travels

Travel our Earth;
learn its worth, of
its birth, and more.

Sleek, Smart and Social Swimmers

Dolphins social in their pod,
Feasting on herring and cod.
Agile, smart, and playful, too,
Swim shallows of ocean blue.

Using echolocation
To find squids; stray crustacean?
Half dolphin's brain stays awake;
Oversees each breath they take.

Taught through Trails

Hiking old trails or new, I always learn
Something else about nature,
Life, peace, and myself, too.

New Approaches

In times of concern it helps sometimes to view things with new approaches.

"Rubbernecks" in Action
Cause Us More Distraction

Why do we slow down
To stare at car accidents,
Which make more likely?

Chapter 6

Resources and Support

"Believe you can and you're halfway there."
"Keep your eyes on the stars and your feet on the ground."
—BOTH QUOTES ATTRIBUTED TO THEODORE ROOSEVELT

THIS CHAPTER IS INTENDED to be a brief compilation of resources (e.g., websites) and support (e.g., books) to assist you in writing quality poetry. It is by no means an exhaustive list. Each item is listed in alphabetical order. Each resource (website) and a brief description of it is provided to help you quickly determine which might be the most relevant for your need(s). The books are largely self-explanatory based on their titles.

Resources (websites):

1. Academy of American Poets: According to its website, "Founded in 1934 in New York City, the Academy of American Poets is the nation's largest membership-based nonprofit organization advocating for American poets and poetry. Its mission is to support American poets at all stages

of their careers and to foster the appreciation of contemporary poetry." Visitors can sign up for free for a poem-a-day. Website: https://www.poets.org/

2. Dictionary.com and Thesaurus.com: These are exactly what their names imply, and although they reside on adjacent tabs, they are both sponsored by Dictionary.com. Website: https://www.dictionary.com

3. English Oxford Living Dictionaries: This free site seems to be a relatively comprehensive source of assistance regarding the English language. It features a dictionary, thesaurus, and some grammar, punctuation, spelling, usage, and writing help. Website: https://en.oxforddictionaries.com

4. Folger Digital Texts: The Folger Shakespeare Library is the largest collection of Shakespearian items in the world. Based on texts from this library, over three dozen Shakespearian plays, as well as 154 sonnets and several other poems, are available free to copy or download. Website: https://www.folgerdigitaltexts.org

5. The Haiku Foundation: According to its website, the mission of The Haiku Foundation (THF) is to "archive our first century of English-language haiku, to expand possibilities for our second, and to seek active exchange with other haiku languages and cultures around the world." Features include a digital library, haiku registry by author's last name, and haiku education resources, among others. Website: https://www.thehaikufoundation.org

6. How Many Syllables: This free site allows the visitor to key in a word, and it provides the syllable count, pronunciation, definition, and words that rhyme with it. Website: https://www.howmanysyllables.com

7. The James G. Martin Center for Academic Renewal: According to its website, "The James G. Martin Center for Academic Renewal is a nonprofit institute dedicated to improving

higher education in North Carolina and the nation. Located in Raleigh, North Carolina, it has been an independent 501(c)(3) organization since 2003. It was known as the John W. Pope Center for Higher Education Policy until January 2017." Click on the Academics tab and do a search on "poetry." Website: https://www.jamesgmartin.center

8. Literary Devices: Definition and Examples of Literary Terms: This free site includes definitions and examples of hundreds of literary terms. Website: https://literarydevices.net

9. MastersInEnglish.org: According to its website, "Masters in English.org is a site dedicated to helping students find the right graduate-level English program. Here you'll find links to accredited degree programs, articles about salary and job prospects, and other useful resources to assist current and prospective graduate students career exploration." Within the "Articles" box is a list of "100 inspiring sites for poets & poetry lovers." Although some sites are mostly relevant to one geographic location and the links to some others did not work, it is still a worthwhile list ,which collectively shows the broad appeal and range of poetic activities taking place. Website: https://mastersinenglish.org

10. Merriam-Webster Dictionary: This free site features a dictionary, thesaurus, word games, a word of the day, and videos on the history and pronunciations of selected words. Website: https://www.merriam-webster.com

11. National Federation of State Poetry Societies: According to its website, "The National Federation of State Poetry Societies (NFSPS) is a non-profit organization, exclusively educational and literary. Its purpose is to recognize the importance of poetry with respect to national cultural heritage. It is dedicated solely to the furtherance of poetry on the national level and serves to unite poets in the bonds of fellowship and understanding." It has an email address for a

point of contact in each of 31 states. Users can enter poetry contests for a small fee. Website: https://www.nfsps.com

12. New Pages: According to its website, "NewPages.com is news, information, and guides to literary magazines, independent publishers, creative writing programs, alternative periodicals, indie bookstores, writing contests, and more." It also has a blog. Website: https://www.newpages.com

13. The Phrontistery: This is a site focusing on archaic, lost, and obscure words, as well as vocabulary resources such as glossaries by topic. It also has a small section (one tab and some links) on numerals and numeration. Website: http://phrontistery.info (Be cautioned that this may not be a secure website.)

14. PoemHunter.com: If you can ignore the cookies and pop-ups, this is a decent poetry site. Its Top 500 Poems and Top 500 Poets features make this website worth exploring. It also has a "Quotations from Famous People" section which includes multiple quotes from 100 people. A member area allows subscribers to submit poems. Website: https://www.poemhunter.com

15. The Poetry Center at Smith College: Founded in 1997, the Poetry Center's mission is to bring to Smith College's campus (located in Northampton, Massachusetts) a succession of poets of national and international stature. The poetry readings are open to students as well as community members. Smith College is the alma mater of the notable late poet, Sylvia Plath. Website: https://www.smith.edu/poetrycenter

16. Poetry Foundation: The Poetry Foundation is based in Chicago, Illinois. According to its website, "The Poetry Foundation, publisher of Poetry magazine, is an independent literary organization committed to a vigorous presence for poetry in our culture. It exists to discover and celebrate the best poetry and to place it before the largest possible

audience." It features free poetry for children and teens, an audio poem of the day, articles and guides to poetry and prose, and more. You can visit the office and its 30,000-volume library. Website: https://www.poetryfoundation.org

17. Poetry Society of America: Poetry Society of America (PSA) is based in New York City. Founded in 1910, according to its website, the mission of the PSA is "is to build a larger and more diverse audience for poetry, to encourage a deeper appreciation of the vitality and breadth of poetry in the cultural conversation, to support poets through an array of programs and awards, and to place poetry at the crossroads of American life." Website: https://www.poetrysociety.org/psa

18. PoetrySoup is an online community of poets of all abilities and experience. It offers free and paid memberships. It features a number of free tools such as a poetry dictionary and thesaurus, grammar checker, and syllable counter. Members may enter any of several dozen free poetry contests taking place at any time. Numerous member poems are featured, as well as works of famous poems. Website: https://www.poetrysoup.com

19. Poets & Writers: Founded in 1970, this organization is based in New York City but also has offices in California and Florida. According to its website, the mission of Poets & Writers is "to foster the professional development of poets and writers, to promote communication throughout the literary community, and to help create an environment in which literature can be appreciated by the widest possible public." It publishes *Poets & Writers Magazine* bimonthly, has writing contests, sponsors grants, and more. Website: https://www.pw.org

20. The Poets Garret: Based in Australia, this site features a wide range of types of poetry, including international poetry, and examples of them. A half-dozen literary references are also

provided. Website: www.thepoetsgarret.com (Be cautioned that this may not be a secure website.)

21. Poets House: Poets House is based in New York City. According to its website, "Poets House is a national poetry library and literary center that invites poets and the public to step into the living tradition of poetry." It has a blog and resources for children, teens, and adults, exhibits, and more. Website: https://poetshouse.org

22. Rhyme Zone: This is a free, online rhyming dictionary and thesaurus. You can use it to find rhymes, near-rhymes, synonyms, antonyms, definitions, correct spelling, and more for words you key in. Website: https://www.rhymezone.com

23. Syllable Counter: This is a free online tool. You type in a word or sentence, and it counts the total number of syllables. The website's owner cautions, "It uses a simple algorithm to calculate the total number of syllables, so it may not be entirely accurate all the time." Website: https://syllablecounter.net

24. 32 Poems: Based in Washington, Pennsylvania, 32 Poems is published in July and December and accepts unsolicited poetry throughout the year, as well as simultaneous submissions. For online submissions, there is a $3 per poem reading fee, which is waived for paying subscribers; however, they also accept fee-free submissions via mail. There is free, partial access to back issues for casual visitors. Contributors get $25 per poem and two copies of the issue in which their work appears. Website: http://32poems.com (Be cautioned that this is not a secure website.)

Support (books):

1. Asimov, Isaac, and Janet Asimov. *How to Enjoy Writing: A Book of Aid and Comfort*. New York: Walker, 1987.

Resources and Support

2. Espy, Willard R. *Words to Rhyme With: Updated Edition.* New York: Checkmark Books, 2001.

3. Janzer, Anne. *The Writer's Process: Getting Your Brain in Gear.* Mountain View, CA: Cuesta Park Consulting, 2016.

4. Kemper, Dave, Patrick Sebranek, and Verne Meyer. *Writers Inc.* Wilmington, MA: Houghton Mifflin, 2001.

5. King, Stephen. *On Writing: A Memoir of the Craft.* 10th anniversary ed. New York: Scribner, 2010.

6. O'Reilly, James, Larry Habegger, and Sean O'Reilly, eds. *The Best Travel Writing.* Vol. 9. Palo Alto, CA: Solas House, 2012.

7. *The Oxford Dictionary of Synonyms and Antonyms: Oxford Quick Reference.* 3rd ed. Oxford: Oxford University Press, 2014.

8. *Publication Manual of the American Psychological Association.* 6th ed. Washington, DC: American Psychological Association, 2010.

9. Spatt, Brenda. *Writing from Sources.* 8th ed. Boston: Bedford/St. Martin's, 2011.

10. Strunk, William, Jr. and E. B. White. *The Elements of Style.* 4th ed. Boston, Allyn and Bacon, 2000.

11. Weldon, Amy E. *The Writer's Eye: Observation and Inspiration for Creative Writers.* London: Bloomsbury, 2018.

12. Wood, James. *How Fiction Works.* New York: Picador, 2008.

Selected Glossary

3-Cubed: Invented by poet Bartholomew Williams in 2016, this form of rhyming poetry consists of three total stanzas, consisting of three lines each. Each line has three syllables, and either successive (e.g., a couplet) or alternating lines must rhyme. The name of this rhyming form of poetry is based on its requirements of three stanzas of three lines each, with each line having three syllables (i.e., 3 stanzas x 3 lines x 3 syllables = 27 total syllables = 3-cubed = 27). For examples, see "Carnival," "Games and Sports," and "Volunteers" on pages 75, 76, and 77, respectively.

4-Cubed: Invented by poet Bartholomew Williams in 2016, this form of rhyming poetry consists of four total stanzas, consisting of four lines each. Each line has four syllables, and either successive (e.g., a couplet) or alternating lines must rhyme. The name of this rhyming form of poetry is based on its requirements of four stanzas of four lines each, with each line having four syllables (i.e., 4 stanzas x 4 lines x 4 syllables = 64 total syllables = 4-cubed = 64). For examples, see "Baseball—Good Call!" and "Leave it out There" on pages 78 and 80, respectively.

5-Cubed: Invented by poet Bartholomew Williams in 2016, this form of rhyming poetry consists of five total stanzas, consisting of five lines each. Each line has five syllables, and either successive (e.g., a couplet) or alternating lines must rhyme. The name of this rhyming form of poetry is based on its requirements of five

Selected Glossary

stanzas of five lines each, with each line having five syllables (i.e., 5 stanzas x 5 lines x 5 syllables = 125 total syllables = 5-cubed = 125). For examples, see "Creative Desire" and "Willingness to Teach" on pages 81 and 82, respectively.

6-Cubed: Invented by poet Bartholomew Williams in 2016, this form of rhyming poetry consists of six total stanzas, consisting of six lines each. Each line has six syllables, and either successive (e.g., a couplet) or alternating lines must rhyme. The name of this rhyming form of poetry is based on its requirements of six stanzas of six lines each, with each line having six syllables (i.e., 6 stanzas x 6 lines x 6 syllables = 216 total syllables = 6-cubed = 216). For an example, see "Drive-in Movie Memories" on page 83.

7-Cubed: Invented by poet Bartholomew Williams in 2016, this form of rhyming poetry consists of seven total stanzas, consisting of seven lines each. Each line has seven syllables, and either successive (e.g., a couplet) or alternating lines must rhyme. The name of this rhyming form of poetry is based on its requirements of seven stanzas of seven lines each, with each line having seven syllables (i.e., 7 stanzas x 7 lines x 7 syllables = 343 total syllables = 7-cubed = 343). For an example, see "The Allure of Lighthouses" on page 85.

8-Cubed: Invented by poet Bartholomew Williams in 2016, this form of rhyming poetry consists of eight total stanzas, consisting of eight lines each. Each line has eight syllables, and either successive (e.g., a couplet) or alternating lines must rhyme. The name of this rhyming form of poetry is based on its requirements of eight stanzas of eight lines each, with each line having eight syllables (i.e., 8 stanzas x 8 lines x 8 syllables = 512 total syllables = 8-cubed = 512). For an example, see "Admiring Heavenly Bodies" on page 87.

Selected Glossary

9-Cubed: Invented by poet Bartholomew Williams in 2016, this form of rhyming poetry consists of nine total stanzas, consisting of nine lines each. Each line has nine syllables, and either successive (e.g., a couplet) or alternating lines must rhyme. The name of this rhyming form of poetry is based on its requirements of nine stanzas of nine lines each, with each line having nine syllables (i.e., 9 stanzas x 9 lines x 9 syllables = 729 total syllables = 9-cubed = 729). For an example, see "Storms Around the World" on page 90.

A

ABC: This is a form of poetry in which every word begins with a successive letter of the alphabet, starting with A. The first word of the second line begins with the letter B, and so on. Alternatively, ABC has sometimes been described as a five-line poem that portrays a picture, feeling, or mood. The first four lines are composed of words, phrases, or clauses—and the first word of each line is in alphabetical order from the first word. The fifth line is one sentence, and it can start with any letter. For examples, see "A Form of Poetry that Uses ABC" on page 101 and "A Birthday Card" on page 122.

Abecedarian: This is a form of a poem in which each succeeding line starts with a successive letter of the alphabet (A, B, C, D, etc.), beginning with A, until the end of the alphabet is reached. It also sometimes referred to as an alphabet poem. For an example, see "ABC's of Appreciation" on page 8.

Acrostcrete: Invented by poet Bartholomew Williams in 2016, this rhyming form of poetry is a hybrid of an acrostic (see below) and a concrete (i.e., a poem that takes the shape of the object it describes) poem, with the further requirement that successive (e.g., a couplet) or alternative lines must rhyme. For examples, see "Books" on page 63, "Fish" on page 64, and "Flag" on page 65.

Selected Glossary

Acrostic: A poem, often in verse, in which the first (typically) or last letters of the lines, or other letters, taken in order form a word, saying, slogan, name, phrase, or motto. For examples, see "Freedom" on page 18, nd "Holly" on pages 27 and 28 respectively, and "Sarah" on page 98.

Alliteration: This is a literary device, primarily of style, in which two or more words having the same first consonant sound occur in close proximity in a series. A key aspect is that alliteration relies on sounds, not the same first letters since that can vary depending on word structure. For an example, see "Grandma" on page 29.

Allusion: An allusion is an indirect and brief reference to a person, thing, place, or idea of cultural, historical, literary, political, spiritual, or other significance. It does not describe at length the person or thing to which it refers, but rather, it is a passing comment. The writer using an allusion expects the reader to recognize and understand it based on the reader's prior knowledge. For an example, the author alludes to Melville's classic book, *Moby Dick*, in "To Uplift, or Live Adrift?" on page 6.

Alternative wording: This is a situation in which the writer selects language to state something which is quite different than more usual or typical ways to state it. An example of alternative wording is using a play on words, and for an example of that, see the sixth line of "To Uplift, or Live Adrift?" on page 6.

Analogy: An analogy is used to compare a thing or idea to another thing that is very different from it. Its goal is to help explain or describe that idea or thing by comparing it to something that is familiar. Examples of analogies are metaphors and similes. For a specific example, the thoughts, questions, and journey of the sailor in "To Uplift, or Live Adrift?" (see page 6) are collectively a metaphor for life.

Selected Glossary

Archaic: This refers to words more commonly used in earlier times but only occasionally today (e.g., to suggest older times as in historical novels, certain ceremonies, etc.).

B

Bio: A poem written about one's own life, personal story(ies), ambitions, personality traits, etc., or those of another person. For an example, see "Across States, Similar Fates" on page 32.

Blank verse: A form of poetry that is characterized by having a regular meter, but no rhyme. The meter most commonly associated with blank verse in English has been iambic pentameter. The iambic pentameter form often approximates the rhythms of speech. Blank verse is different from free verse since free verse does not utilize strict meter. For an example, see "Could Have Rhymed but Doesn't" on page 158.

C

Caricature: This is a drawing, picture, description, etc., that significantly exaggerates some of the peculiarities or uniquely identifying features of a person or a thing. Political cartoons often make use of caricatures.

Carpe diem: The is a type of poem that encourages people to use the time they have now to accomplish significant things. It is Latin for, "Seize the day." For examples, see "Sunrise!" on page 12 and "Supersonic!" on page 120.

Chastushka: A form of traditional Russian poetry, a chastushka consists of a single quatrain in trochaic tetrameter with an abab or abcb rhyme scheme. This type of poem is typically humorous, ironic, or satirical. Chastushkas can be put to music as well,

Selected Glossary

sometimes with accordion accompaniment. This type of poem is comparable to, but one line shorter than, limericks found in British culture. For an example, see "Less Costs More at the Store" on page 171.

Choka: A choka has alternating lines of five and seven syllables (e.g., 5-7-7-5-7-7-5-5-7) and ends with an extra line of seven syllables. The choka, or long poem, is an intricate form of Japanese poetry. For an example, see "Canadian Geese: Still Roam or Stay Home?" on page 161.

Cinquain: A traditional cinquain is based on a syllable count. Line 1 has two syllables. Line 2 has four syllables. Line 3 has six syllables. Line 4 has eight syllables. Line 5 has two 2 syllables. The total syllable count is 22. Today's cinquains are based on a word count of words of a certain type and purpose. Line 1 has one word, a noun, which is a title or name of the subject. Line 2 has two words, adjectives, describing the title. Line 3 has three words, verbs, describing an action related to the title. Line 4 consists of four words describing a feeling about the title and is a complete sentence. Line 5 has one word, which refers back to the title. For an example of a traditional cinquain, see "Sometimes" on page 39.

Clerihew: A clerihew is a specific type of short humorous verse, often with the following features: It is biographical and typically whimsical, portraying the subject from an unusual point of view, but it is hardly ever satirical, abusive or obscene. It consists of four lines of irregular length for a humorous effect. The first line consists solely, or almost solely, of a well-known person's name. For an example, see "An Eyebrow-raising Key to Electricity" about Benjamin Franklin on page 119.

Cliché: This is a trite, stereotyped expression, sentence, or phrase that often expresses a popular or common thought or idea that has lost originality, freshness, and impact through overuse.

Selected Glossary

Concrete: A concrete poem is one that takes the shape of the object it describes. This is different from a shape poem because a shape poem does not have to take the shape of the object it describes. For examples, see "Stars' Sharing" and "Tree" on pages 131 and 132, respectively.

Couplet: A couplet is a rhyming stanza consisting of two lines, or else a pair of lines of a verse that forms a unit, since couplets can rhyme but do not have to. For examples, see "Soaring Symbol of Strength" (p. 21), "Fair Thrills" (p. 100), "One Ancient Wall Stands Above All" (p. 172), and "Sleek, Smart, and Social Swimmers" (p. 176).

Crystalline: This is a two-line image poem, usually with a title, in which euphony is the key element. Each line may have eight or nine syllables, but the total number of syllables is seventeen. For an example, see "Subtle Call of Waterfall" on page 133.

D

Deca: Invented by poet Bartholomew Williams in 2017, this form of rhyming poetry consists of 10 total lines of 10 syllables each, for 100 syllables in all. Successive (e.g., a couplet) or alternating lines must rhyme. It can consist of one to five stanzas. Its meter can be iambic pentameter but doesn't have to be. For examples, see "Decades of Distraction," "Deliverance at Dunkirk," and "Friends for Different Ends" on pages 66, 67, and 68, respectively.

Dialect: a variety of the same language that is distinguished in spoken form from other varieties of that same language by features of phonology, vocabulary, grammar, and by its use among a group of speakers who are set off from others geographically or socially.

Selected Glossary

Diamante: A seven-line poem shaped like a diamond, a diamante progresses from the subject at the top of the diamond to another totally different, and occasionally opposite, subject at the bottom. For an example, see "Inquisitiveness" on page 154.

Double entendre: A word or expression used in a certain context such that it could be interpreted in two ways, especially when one meaning is risqué. See the use of double entendre in "A Taxing Experience" on page 110.

Dramatic monologue: A type of lengthy lyric poem in which a character in fiction or in history delivers a long speech explaining his or her feelings, actions, motives, or thoughts. It is similar to a narration by that character. For examples, see "My Inner Voice—Supportive Choice" and "Patriotic Pursuits" on pages 13 and 22, respectively.

E

Elegy: A poem of grief, mourning, or sadness about the death of an individual, as well as a reflection on what the deceased's life meant to the writer. For an example, see "Lament from the Living" on page 145.

Enclosed rhyme: A poem that utilizes a rhyme scheme a-b-b-a (i.e., the first and fourth lines rhyme, as do the second and third lines). For an example, see "Antarctica—Cold, High, and Dry" on page 166.

Environmental poetry: The theme of environmental poetry, which takes many forms, focuses on nature, being good stewards of the Earth and its natural resources, and respecting, conserving, protecting, and restoring the air, land, and water. Examples are "Silently Seeking Nature's Voice" (p. 34), "Connecting with Nature"

Selected Glossary

(p. 35), "Glaciers are Weeping" (p. 37), "Framework of the Forest" (p. 40), "Giant Sequoia—King of All Trees!" (p. 41), "Fish" (p. 64), "Storms Around the World" (p. 90), "Antarctica—Cold, High, and Dry" (p. 166), "Northern Necessities" (p. 167), and "Living Gratefully" (p. 174).

Epic poem: This is a significant poem that relates the story of a heroic figure. It is a widely defined genre of poetry and one of the key forms of narrative literature. The subject of this substantial, continuous narrative may be a heroic or mythological person or group of persons.
The Iliad and *The Odyssey* by the ancient Greek poet, Homer, are two well-known examples.

Etheree: Invented in the late 20th century by the late poet, Etheree Taylor Armstrong, an Etheree consists of ten lines of unmetered and unrhymed verse. The first line has one syllable, the second line two syllables, and so forth, through the 10-syllable tenth line. The total syllable count is 55. Variations include the reverse Etheree (i.e., the first line has 10 syllables, the second line nine syllables, etc.) and the stacked Etheree (i.e., two Etherees on top of each other, totaling 20 lines and 110 syllables). For examples, see "Poem Could Be an Etheree" (p. 103), "Fear" (p. 146), and "Free—Basic to First Amendment" (p. 156).

Euphemism: the substitution of a mild, indirect, or vague expression or word for one thought to be too offensive, harsh, blunt, or embarrassing.

F

Fibonacci: In a Fibonacci poem, the number of syllables in each line has to equal the sum of the syllables in the two previous lines. Therefore, starting with 0 and 1, they are added together to get the

Selected Glossary

next number, which is 1. Thus, the first line has one syllable. The second line also has one syllable. The third line has two syllables. Fibonacci numbers are: 0, 1, 1, 2, 3, 5, 8, 13, 21, 34, etc. For an example, see "Road Trips" on page 130.

Footle: A footle has two lines, with two syllables per line. It is a trochaiac monometer poem with an integral title suitable for witty, humorous, light, topical, and/or pertinent verse. For examples, see "Rhyme Time" and "Lighten Up" on page 102, and "Final Footle" on page 162. For examples of footle series, see "Gaining Ground" (p. 116) and "Elusive Poet" (p. 117).

G

Ghazal: This poetic form, pronounced "guzzle," consists of five to 15 couplets which share a rhyme and a refrain. For an example, the second line of each couplet may all rhyme with each other. For an example, see "Aesthetic Africa" on page 168.

H

Haiku: A traditional Japanese haiku consists of three lines. The first line has five syllables, the second line has seven syllables, and the last line has five syllables. For examples, see "Stargazing Reflections" (p. 14), "Connecting with Nature" (p. 35), "POW's Paradox" (p. 144), and "Northern Necessities" (p. 167).

I

Iambic pentameter: This is a meter in poetry, consisting of lines with five (therefore "pentameter") iambs—or "feet"—in which the iamb is the dominant foot (hence "Iambic"). An iamb is a metrical foot comprised of an unstressed (or short) syllable followed by a stressed (or long) syllable, like so—da DUM. Iambic pentameter involves five meters—da DUM da DUM da DUM da DUM da DUM. Slight or occasional departures from either pattern are allowed, such as one extra or missing syllable. For examples, see "To Be with Her" (p. 26) and "The Chill of Autumn, the Warmth of Romance" (p. 150).

Imagery: the use of words that help "paint" mental images for the readers of poetry and other literature. For an example, see "The Promise of Spring" on page 47.

Inspirational poetry: This is high-quality poetry that evokes enthusiasm, motivation, and higher ideals in its readers. It is often both moving and memorable, and it enlivens those who read it. See Chapter 1, especially its first 23 poems, for examples.

Internal rhyme: a rhyme created by two or more words in the same line of verse or a rhyme created by words within two or more lines of a verse. For an example, see "Road Trips" on page 130.

Irony: Irony is the use of words to convey meaning in a poem or story that varies from or is the opposite of its meaning in reality, with the outcome often different than what the reader anticipated or hoped for. A footle or footle series can be an effective form for conveying irony. See, For an example, "Elusive Poet" on page 117.

J

Jueju: This form of Chinese poetry consists of a matched pair of couplets, or a quatrain, with each line consisting of five or seven syllables. The five-syllable form is called *wujue* (For examples, see "Soaring Symbol of Strength" (p. 21), "One Ancient Wall Stands Above All" (p. 172), and "Sleek, Smart, and Social Swimmers" (p. 176)), and the seven-syllable form is called *qijue*.

K

Kimo: A post-haiku poetic form, a kimo consists of three lines of 10, 7, and 6 syllables. This form of poetry was invented in Israel. For an example, see "Taught Through Trails" on page 177.

L

Lanterne: A type of poem that has one syllable in the first line, two syllables in the second line, three syllables in the third line, four syllables in the fourth line, and one syllable in the fifth line that relates to the first word of the poem. For an example, see "Farms" on page 134.

Light verse: Light verse is poetry that aims at being humorous. For an example, see "A Taxing Experience" on page 110.

Limerick: A limerick is a five-line, frequently humorous, poem with a strict meter or distinctive rhythm. The first, second, and fifth lines of each have seven to ten syllables and rhyme with one another. The third and fourth lines of each have five to seven syllables and rhyme with each other. The rhyme scheme is usually "aabba." For an example, see "Seasick" on page 109.

Lyric: An easy-flowing form of poetry, expressing the feelings and thoughts of the writer, that is amenable to being set to music.

M

Metaphor: a figure of speech in which a term or phrase is applied to something to which it is not literally applicable in order to suggest a resemblance. The thoughts, questions, and journey of the sailor in "To Uplift, or Live Adrift?" (p. 6) are collectively a metaphor for life.

SELECTED GLOSSARY

Meter: In poetry, meter is a unit of rhythm. It is a pattern of stressed (longer) and unstressed (shorter) syllables in verse, including poetry. Stressed, or emphasized, syllables are the hard—or long—component of a word, and unstressed syllables are the soft or shorter portions. Meter helps provide a rhythm to the poem, which is particularly apparent when the poem is read aloud. Poems in English can utilize five different types of meter.

Monoku: A monoku is a haiku in a single horizontal line. For an example, see "New Approaches" on page 178.

Monorhyme: In monorhyme poetry, the end of each line rhymes with every other line. This form of poetry is common in Latin and Arabic.

Motif: a dominant or recurring subject, theme, idea, feature, etc., especially in literary, artistic, or musical work.

N

Narrative: Narrative poetry tells a story. In a broad sense, epic poetry is a form of narrative poetry; however, narrative poetry also includes works of poetry on a smaller scale. For examples, see "Maritime Missions" (p. 135) and "'Sailing' in Space to a Lunar Landing" (p. 138).

Ninette: A ninette consists of nine lines, each increasing in one syllable, then after the midpoint (line 5), decreasing again. The form, when centered on a page, looks like a paper lantern. The first and last word may be the same, antonyms, or synonyms. For an example, see "Some of Life's Phases—In a Few Phrases" on page 159.

O

Obscure: not known about or seen; concealed; uncertain.

Ode: A lengthy lyric poem, typically expressing emotion and addressed to someone or something. A classic ode is one that has three parts—the strophe, the antistrophe, and the epode.

Onomatopoeia: the use of imitative and naturally suggestive words (i.e., a sound associated with what is named) for rhetorical, dramatic, or poetic effect.

Ottava rima: This is Italian poetry. In English, an ottava rima stanza is comprised of eight lines, usually written in iambic pentameter. Each stanza consists of three rhymes following the rhyme scheme a-b-a-b-a-b-c-c. For an example, see "The Southern Tier of Western Hemisphere" on page 170.

Oxymoron: a figure of speech in which two seemingly opposite concepts or actions are joined to create an ironic effect.

P

Pantoum: This is a rare form of poetry comparable to a villanelle. It consists of a series of four-line stanzas, in which the second and fourth lines of the first stanza are the first and third lines of the next. This pattern is continued for any number of stanzas, except for the final stanza, which differs in the repeating pattern. The first and third lines of the last stanza are the second and fourth of the penultimate (next to the last stanza); the first line of the poem is the last line of the final stanza, and the third line of the first stanza is the second of the final. When written in an ideal way, the meaning of lines shifts when they are repeated, although the words remain exactly the same. This can be achieved by shifting

Selected Glossary

punctuation, punning, or simply contextualizing again. For an example, see "Sunrise!" on page 12.

Parable: a short allegorical story designed to illustrate or teach some truth, spiritual principle, or moral lesson.

Parallelism: This is the use of words or phrases in a sentence that are grammatically similar or similar in structure, meaning, sound, meter, or action. This approach adds rhythm and balance to phrases, lines and stanzas in poems. For an example, see "Some Simple Joys" on page 149.

Patriotic poetry: Poetry focusing on an individual or group's positive pride in their home country, its institutions, history, accomplishments, values, traditions, advancements, etc. For examples, see "Freedom" (p. 18), "Freedom in Flight" (p. 19), "Soaring Symbol of Strength" (p. 21), "Patriotic Pursuits" (p. 22), and "Free—Basic to First Amendment" (p. 156).

Personification: A form of poetry in which human characteristics are attributed to non-human things such as animals, concepts or abstract ideas, objects, and places. Personification provides a poet a means by which to ascribe life, emotions, movement, and other human characteristics to non-human things, in an effort to make more sense of the world. For an example, see "Glaciers are Weeping" on page 37.

Pleiades: The first word in each line begins with the same letter as the title in this seven-line form of poetry, which was created in 1999 by Craig Tigerman, Lead Editor of Sol Magazine. Pleiades (a.k.a. the Seven Sisters) is the Greek name for the seven-star cluster in the Taurus constellation. For examples, see "Holistic" (six syllables per line version) on page 151, "Innovation" (seven syllables per line version) on page 152, and "Willpower" (seven syllables per line) on page 153.

Selected Glossary

Prose: Prose is writing that is different from typical poetry by its greater variety of rhythm and its closer resemblance to the patterns of everyday speech. The word "prose" is derived from the Latin term *prosa*, meaning "straightforward." This demonstrates the kind of writing that prose embodies, unadorned with stylistic devices. Prose writing is typically adopted for the description of facts or the discussion of ideas. Therefore, it is suitable for magazines, newspapers, encyclopedias, plays, films, papers, philosophy, letters, essays, novels, history, biographies, short stories, and many other forms of written communication.

Pun: the humorous use of a word or phrase to emphasize or suggest one or more of its different meanings or applications, or the use of words that are alike or nearly alike in sound but different in meaning; a play on words.

Q

Quatrain: A quatrain is a stanza or poem consisting of four lines. In its basic form, the second and fourth lines must rhyme while also having a similar number of syllables. See, for example, "Looking to Sea" on page 11, which consists of six stanzas, each of which is a quatrain.

Questionku: A questionku consists of three lines. The first line has four syllables, the second line has five syllables, and the third line has six syllables. The poem ends with a question. For an example, see "Cosmic Context" on page 173.

R

Repetition: the act of repeating, or doing, saying, or writing something again; repeated action, performance, production, or presentation in order to make the ideas clearer and more memorable.

Rhyme: A rhyming poem has the repetition of the same or similar sounds of two or more words, often at the end of the line. A rhyme scheme is the pattern taken by these rhyming words. For instance, alternating lines of poetry that rhyme follow the rhyme scheme a-b-a-b.

Rispetto: A rispetto poem generally consists of eight 11-syllable lines. Early on, the rhyme scheme was typically a-b-a-b-a-b-c-c. Later on, the pattern a-b-a-b-c-c-d-d became more prevalent. Other versions have been written, as well. For an example of the earlier rhyme scheme, see "Recreational Retreat" on page 160.

Rondeau: A rondeau is a French form of poetry with 15 lines written on two rhymes. Variations may consist of 10 or 13 lines. A Rondeau makes use of refrains, repeated according to a set pattern. It is sometimes seen as a challenge to put together these refrains in ways that add meaning to the poem in efficient and impactful ways. A rondeau is comprised of thirteen full lines of eight syllables, plus two refrains (which are half lines, each of four syllables), employing, collectively, only three rhymes. For an example, see "A Wonder Down Under" on page 169.

S

Sarcasm: a literary and rhetorical device intended to deride a person, group, institution, or segment of society.

Satirical poetry: This type of poetry is used to call attention to the foolishness, rudeness, and/or corruption of an individual, group, segment of the population, or society as a whole. For an example, see "Where Have Good Manners Gone?" on page 157.

Selected Glossary

Sausage poetry: It is believed sausage poetry was created by a poet in the Sheboygan, Wisconsin area in the early 2000's. It consists of at least eight words, one per line vertically. The last letter of each word must be the first letter of the next. For examples, see "An Eagle Goes Fishing" (p. 42) and "A Hot Date" (p. 118).

Senryu: This is a short Japanese-style poem, similar to a haiku in structure. However, senryus are often darkly humorous or cynical and tend to be about human faux pas, whereas haikus are more serious and frequently nature-themed. For an example, see "'Rubbernecks' in Action, Cause Us More Distraction" on page 179.

Serial poetry: Invented by poet Bartholomew Williams in 2015, this is a series of three or more rhyming poems, each of which can stand alone, but as a combined series, tell one larger story. Also, there is a separate overall title for each series of poems that ties the series together. See the three examples of serial poetry that lead off Chapter 2. They are "Spring, Summer, and Two More: Seasons Cycle Through Four" (four poems, which start on page 47), "Raining, Draining, Life-sustaining" (three poems, which begin on page 55), and "Five Phases of Our Lives" (five poems, which commence on page 58).

Shape poetry: Written in the shape or form of an object, a shape poem does not have to take the form of the object it describes.

Simile: a figure of speech in which two unlike things are explicitly compared in order to more dramatically or memorably describe the object of the comparison (e.g., quiet as a mouse).

Social commentary: the act of using rhetorical means to bring attention to and opine on issues in society.

Selected Glossary

Sonnet: In the classic sense, a sonnet is a lyric poem that is 14 lines in length and usually has one or more conventional rhyme schemes, such as rhyming couplet. Typically, three four-line stanzas are followed by one concluding two-line stanza. For an example, see "To Be with Her" on page 26.

Stanza: an arrangement of a certain number of lines, usually four or more, sometimes having a fixed length, meter, or rhyme scheme, forming adivision of a poem.

Syllable: an uninterrupted segment of speech consisting of a vowel sound, a diphthong, or a syllabic consonant, with or without preceding or following consonant sounds.

Symbolism: the art or practice of representing things by such symbols as an object, characters, or words, or of investing things with a symbolic meaning or character.

T

Tail-rhyme: This French form consists of two rhymes. First, there is typically a rhyming couplet of eight syllables and then a third and shorter line. The fourth and fifth lines are another couplet that rhymes with the first couplet. The sixth, shorter line rhymes with the third line. That suggests a rhyme scheme of a-a-b-c-c-b. For an example, see "Careful Concerning Contracts" on page 155.

Tanka: A Japanese poem of five lines, the first and third composed of five syllables and the others seven. In Japanese, tanka is often written in one straight line, but in English and other languages, we usually divide the lines into the five syllabic units: 5-7-5-7-7. For an example, see "Living Gratefully" on page 174.

Selected Glossary

Tercet: a three-lined verse rhyming together or connected by rhyme with an adjacent tercet.

Tetrameter: a verse of four feet (i.e., meters, or units of poetic rhythm).

Than-Bauk: Conventionally a witty saying or epigram, a Than-Bauk is a three line "climbing rhyme" poem that originated in Burma. Each line has four syllables. The rhyme is on the fourth syllable of the first line, the third syllable of the second line, and the second syllable of the third line. For an example, see "Terrestrial Travels" on page 175.

Theme: The theme is the subject of discourse, discussion, meditation, composition, poetry, and other such efforts. It is the overall message of the work.

Title: The distinguishing name of a book, poem, movie, painting, picture, piece of music, or the like is its title. It may be considered essentially the headline for the creative work.

Tragic: refers to, pertaining to, characterized by, or of the nature of tragedy or a bad ending. For examples, see "Ignoring a Warning Left a Nation in Mourning" on page 140 and "*Titanic* Tragedy" on page 142.

Transition: words, phrases, and sentences that provide a connection or "bridge" between ideas, sentences, paragraphs, and other parts of literary works.

U

Utopia: any so-called visionary system of political or social perfection or an ideal place or state. For social commentary on a classic

Selected Glossary

utopian vision, see "Still a Brave New World Ahead—Cloning, Eugenics Not Dead?" on page 147.

V

Vertical monocrostic: This acrostic has one word in each line and spells out some word, saying, slogan, name, phrase, motto, etc. vertically. For an example, see "Stan" on page 99.

Villanelle: A 19-line poem consisting of five tercets and a final quatrain on two rhymes. The first and third lines of the first tercet repeat alternately as a refrain closing the succeeding stanzas and joined as the final couplet of the quatrain. For an example, see "Building Connections" on page 10.

Z

ZYX: Invented by poet Bartholomew Williams in 2015, ZYX is a rhyming, 26-line poem in which the first line starts with a Z, the second line starts with a Y, the third line starts with an X, and each succeeding line starts with a previous letter of the alphabet (e.g., W, V, U, etc.) until the beginning of the alphabet is reached. It may be thought of an Abecedarian poem in reverse. For examples, see "Zest to Travel the 50 States of America" (p. 69), "Some Obscure Meanings Eclipsed; References Archaic, Research Enlightening; Meanings Attached to Them Each Relevant, Still (SOME RARE MATTERS)" (p. 71), and "Ships and Boats from Z to A" (p. 73).

Index of Titles

Title of poem	Page No.
ABC's of Appreciation	8
Across States, Similar Fates	32
Admiring Heavenly Bodies	32
Aesthetic Africa	168
Allure of Lighthouses, The	85
Antarctica—Cold, High, and Dry	166
Arctic Sustenance	165
Autumn Harvest and Last Call of Fall	51
Baseball—Good Call!	78
Beth	27
Birthday Card, A	122
Books	63
Building Connections	10
Camping Trip	128
Canadian Geese: Still Roam or Stay Home?	161
Careful Concerning Contracts	155
Carnival	75
Childhood: Rising Up, Sizing Up	58

Index of Titles

Chill of Autumn, the Warmth of Romance, The	150
Community Creek	123
Connecting with Nature	35
Cosmic Context	173
Could Have Rhymed but Doesn't	158
Creative Desire	81
Dare to Dream!	4
Decades of Distraction	66
Deliverance at Dunkirk	67
Drive-in Movie Memories	83
Eagle Goes Fishing, An	42
Early Middle Age: Calling, Career, and Clan	60
Elderly/Golden Age: Time for Shedding Some Tears, but Still Meaningful Years	62
Elusive Poet	117
Eyebrow-raising Key to Electricity, An	119
Fair Thrills	100
Family Farm	30
Farms	134
Father	25
Fear	146
Final Footle	162
Fish	64
Flag	65
Form of Poetry that Uses ABC, A	101
Framework of the Forest	40
Free—Basic to First Amendment	156
Freedom	18

Index of Titles

Freedom in Flight	19
Friends for Different Ends	68
Gaining Ground	116
Games and Sports	76
Giant Sequoia—King of All Trees!	41
Glaciers are Weeping	37
Grandma	29
Holistic	151
Holly	28
Hot Date, A	118
Ignoring a Warning Left a Nation in Mourning	140
Innovation	152
Inquisitiveness	154
Lament from the Living	145
Late Middle Age: Children Take Flight, a Second Light	61
Leave it out There	80
Less Costs More at the Store	171
Lighten Up	102
Liquid Life	55
Living Gratefully	174
Looking to Sea	11
Maritime Missions	135
Mother	23
My Inner Voice—Supportive Choice	13
New Approaches	178
Northern Necessities	167
One Ancient Wall Stands Above All	172
Patriotic Pursuits	22

Index of Titles

Poem Could Be an Etheree	103
POW's Paradox	144
Promise of Spring, The	47
Ready for the Road	99
Recreational Retreat	160
Rhyme Time	102
Rhythm of the Rain	15
Rivers' Motions Refill Oceans	57
Road Trips	130
Roll to Play	115
Root Beer River	126
'Rubbernecks' in Action, Cause Us More Distraction	179
'Sailing' in Space to a Lunar Landing	138
Sarah	98
Seasick	109
Ships and Boats from Z to A	73
Silently Seeking Nature's Voice	34
Skies Raining, Fields Draining	56
Sleek, Smart and Social Swimmers	176
Soaring Symbol of Strength	21
Solitude in Academia	16
Some Obscure Meanings Eclipsed; References Archaic, Research Enlightening; Meanings Attached to Them Each Relevant, Still (SOME RARE MATTERS)	71
Some of Life's Phases—In a Few Phrases	159
Some Simple Joys	149
Sometimes	39
Southern Tier of Western Hemisphere, The	170

Index of Titles

Stan	99
Stargazing Reflections	14
Stars' Sharing	131
Still a Brave New World Ahead—Cloning, Eugenics Not Dead?	147
Storms Around the World	90
Subtle Call of Waterfall	133
Sudden Storm	124
Summer's Allure and Time to Mature	49
Sunrise!	12
Sunshine Café	33
Supersonic!	120
Taught Through Trails	177
Taxing Experience, A	110
Tell Them Now	7
Temporary Space, Personal Place	113
Terrestrial Travels	175
Time	36
Titanic Tragedy	142
To Be with Her	26
To Uplift, or Live Adrift?	6
Tree	132
Up and Down, Round and Round	112
Volunteers	77
What am I?	114
Where Have Good Manners Gone?	157
Willingness to Teach	82
Willpower	153

Index of Titles

Winter Dormancy, Death, and Deliverance	53
Wonder Down Under, A	169
You Are Worth It	5
You Can Do It!	3
Young Adulthood: Finding One's Path	59
Zest to Travel the 50 States of America	69

Index of First Lines

First line of poem	Page No.
A birthday card when I was but a kid,	122
A creative spark	81
A dozen years into twentieth century;	142
A graceful eagle soaring free;	19
A human feat among all,	172
A land of much diverse biology;	170
A miser by any measure,	110
A run on the trail, a walk in the park;	149
A treetop's leafy crown;	132
A young man shipped out on the sea;	109
Africa—Serengeti—its vast plains;	168
After gray skies rain, fields drain.	56
Ah, sunrise! A great time to seize the day!	12
An abecedarian poem—one should not forget,	101
An expectant glow and a radiant smile;	23
An oak stands its ground for many a decade;	40
Appreciate others in ways that fit their needs.	8
As	131

Index of First Lines

At 18 comes tech school, military, college?	59
At 36-plus, talent and treasure gained;	60
Beautiful person who's second to none;	27
Benjamin Franklin, to prove lightning held electricity,	119
Bi-covered treasure	63
Birth	159
By many names—storms around the world;	90
Car running well, its tank full; he slept much, so mind not dull.	99
Co-leader keeping a family strong;	25
Dare to dream all things mild to mighty,	4
Dawn had come, the sun was out;	120
Ditching high-tech toys,	35
Dolphins social in their pod,	176
During the time before children's memories last,	58
Eagle	42
Every day and in every way you are worth it.	5
Example here of blank verse poetry;	158
Excited—	118
Farms	134
Fear,	146
First whistle sounds,	80
Five years into the U.S. program of space shuttle flight,	140
For a nation, state, city, cause, other;	65
For thousands of years, ice giants were sleeping.	37
Free -	156
Freedom is never free.	18
Freshwater or marine;	64

Index of First Lines

Friends come in many types and times in life.	68
Games and sports	76
Games, food, rides,	75
Giant Sequoia, king of all trees!	41
"Give me liberty, or give me death!"	22
Graceful eagle freely soars	21
Heavy, gray skies are weeping;	55
Hiking old trails or new, I always learn	177
Holidays inspired the name we bestowed upon you;	28
Holistic—complete view:	151
Homer, Aristotle, Hobbes, Locke, Goethe, and Crane;	16
Hot summer days yield to the cool autumn breeze;	51
I	130
I may have eyes, but I have no ability to see.	114
I ponder my existence beyond the breakers,	6
I struggle nobly to describe my love.	26
I walk along the ocean shore	11
I watched a cartoon movie	83
If you appreciate others, tell them now,	7
In 1492, Columbus set sail on the seas;	138
In silence I seek nature's voice,	34
In times of concern it helps sometimes to view things with new	178
In times of trouble, face of fear, and other stress,	13
Inquisitiveness,	154
Inspiration, need, or both;	152
Instead of fractures, let me build connections,	10
Is government control of humans' birth, aging, and dying	147

Index of First Lines

Land of gum trees, circled by seas;	169
Last 20 years—decades of distraction;	66
Last continent to which humans did divert;	166
Late May to early June 1940;	67
Lighthouse—sentinel seaside;	85
Looking forward to a relaxing weekend afternoon,	126
Made rhyme	102
Maritime missions—real and varying;	135
Migratory birds	161
My daughter was growing up, becoming more independent;	33
My unknown older brother, I often think of you.	145
No rhyme	117
Not really looking for romance that fall,	150
Oh, my! Where have good manners gone these days,	157
One man born in Schenectady, New York, before the Great Depression;	32
Paddling a kayak, rivers and great sea call;	165
Prisoner of war [POW]	144
Providing a safe, steady place	113
Ran fast	116
Reached end;	162
Read each contract, though you might squint.	155
Retirement generates both comfort and query;	62
Roll me, and with luck, you just might win;	115
Sea—giver of food;	167
Second	99
Sensing the amazing night sky	87
Shopper said to corner vendor,	171

Index of First Lines

Sincere in caring about her peers;	98
Sometimes	39
Somewhere among this fair's iron hills,	100
Spring's promise transitions to summer solstice;	49
Stargazing, I sense	14
Stealthy five decades-plus creep up—age 54;	61
The car's loaded up with tents, sleeping bags, and the rest of our gear;	128
The promise of spring is a time of rebirth.	47
The year long in the tooth, the crops have been gathered;	53
This	103
Time, the great equalizer, yet mastered by none;	36
To my siblings and me while growing up,	30
Travel our Earth;	175
Trillions of stars;	173
Uptight	102
Visiting Grandma one hot and humid summer day;	124
Volume helps rivers run fast;	57
Voluminous rush of waterfall -	133
Volunteers	77
We can decide to . . .	174
When spring is here,	78
When troubles and turmoil lay their grip on me,	160
While lying in my bed, I leisurely listen	15
Why do we slow down	179
Willingness to teach;	82
Willpower, or self-control,	153
With your sweet smile and thoughtful touch;	29

INDEX OF FIRST LINES

Years ago, when my friends and I were just boys;	123
You can do it—I believe in you!	3
You can walk the dog with me,	112
Zest-filled to travel to all the states in our great nation;	69
Zille—flat-bottomed boat, may have a hut amidships;	73
Zoetic, an adjective, pertains to life;	71

About the Frontispiece Photos

Upper left:	Afternoon sun rays stream through clouds near Yosemite National Park in California, USA.
Upper right:	Upper and Lower Yosemite Falls in Yosemite National Park.
Lower left:	Oceanfront beach scene on the island of Kauai, Hawaii.
Lower right:	One of the many beautiful trails in Monet's Garden in Giverny, France.

Bibliography

Aristotle. "Aristotle Quotes." BrainyQuote.com. *Accessed August 24, 2018. https://www.brainyquote.com/quotes/aristotle_163785*
Asimov, Isaac, and Janet Asimov. *How to Enjoy Writing: A Book of Aid and Comfort.* New York: Walker, 1987.
Bashō, Matsuo. *The Complete Haiku.* 1st ed. Tokyo: Kodansha International, 2008.
Chaucer, Geoffrey. *The Canterbury Tales.* New York: Barnes & Noble, 2006.
Collins, Billy. "Billy Collins Quotes." BrainyQuote.com. *Accessed August 24, 2018. https://www.brainyquote.com/quotes/billy_collins_715745*
Crane, Stephen. *The Works of Stephen Crane in 10 Volumes Complete: Univ. Virginia edition.* Charlottesville: University of Virginia, 1969–1976.
Dickens, Charles. *Works of Charles Dickens.* New York: Hurd & Houghton, 1869.
Dickinson, Emily. *The Complete Poems of Emily Dickinson,* ed. Thomas H. Johnson. Boston: Little, Brown, 1955.
Ellis, Nelsan. "Nelsan Ellis Quotes." BrainyQuote.com. *Accessed August 24, 2018. https://www.brainyquote.com/quotes/nelsan_ellis_848458*
Espy, Willard R. *Words to Rhyme With: Updated Edition.* New York: Checkmark, 2001.
Frost, Robert. *The Poetry of Robert Frost,* ed. E. C. Lathem. New York: Henry Holt, 1969.
Hemingway, Ernest. *The Complete Short Stories of Ernest Hemingway: The Finca Vigía edition.* New York: Scribner, 1987.
Hendershot, Mary Alice. *Reflections in Poetry and Prose.* New York: Carlton, 1961.
Hesselbein, Frances. "Frances Hesselbein Quotes." BrainyQuote.com. *Accessed August 24, 2018. https://www.brainyquote.com/quotes/frances_hesselbein_903430*
Hobbes, Thomas. *The Complete Works of Thomas Hobbes,* ed. William Molesworth. Abingdon, UK: Routledge, 1993.
Homer. *The Iliad,* trans. Robert Fitzgerald. Garden City, NY: Doubleday, 1975.
Homer. *The Odyssey,* trans. Robert Fitzgerald. Garden City, NY: Doubleday, 1963.

Bibliography

Huxley, Aldous (1932/1946). *Brave New World*. New York: HarperCollins, 2006.

Janzer, Anne. *The Writer's Process: Getting Your Brain in Gear*. Mountain View, CA: Cuesta Park Consulting, 2016.

Keats, John. "John Keats Quotes." BrainyQuote.com. Accessed August 24, 2018. https://www.brainyquote.com/quotes/john_keats_106894

Kemper, Dave, Patrick Sebranek, and Verne Meyer. *Writers Inc*. Wilmington, MA: Houghton Mifflin, 2001.

King, Stephen. *On Writing: A Memoir of the Craft*. 10th anniversary ed. New York: Scribner, 2010.

Locke, John. *The Works of John Locke in Nine Volumes*. 12th ed. London: Rivington, 1824.

Magee Jr., John Gillespie (Pilot Officer, Royal Canadian Air Force, 1941). "High Flight" (a poem which includes the oft-quoted words, "slipped the surly bonds of Earth . . . and touched the face of God").

Manuel, Frank E. *The Age of Reason*. Ithaca, NY: Cornell University Press, 1951.

Melville, Herman. *Moby-Dick* (a.k.a. *The Whale*). London: Richard Bentley, 1851.

O'Reilly, James, Larry Habegger, and Sean O'Reilly, eds. *The Best Travel Writing*. Vol. 9. Palo Alto, CA: Solas House, 2012.

The Oxford Dictionary of Synonyms and Antonyms: Oxford Quick Reference. 3rd ed. Oxford: Oxford University Press, 2014.

Plato. *Apology*, ed. John Burnet. Oxford: Clarendon, 1924. [In this classical work, Plato tells the reader that Socrates uttered, "The unexamined life is not worth living," at his trial for supposed impiety and allegedly corrupting youth. Then, Socrates accepted his sentence and drank deadly hemlock to preserve his principles.]

Poe, Edgar Allan. *Complete Stories and Poems of Edgar Allan Poe*. Garden City, NY: Doubleday, 1966.

Poe, Edgar Allan. "Edgar Allan Poe Quotes." BrainyQuote.com. Accessed August 24, 2018. https://www.brainyquote.com/quotes/edgar_allan_poe_107273

Publication Manual of the American Psychological Association. 6th ed. Washington, DC: American Psychological Association, 2010.

Rampersad, Arnold, and David Roessel, eds. *The Collected Poems of Langston Hughes*. New York: Alfred A. Knopf, 1994.

Robinson, W. Andrew. *Einstein: A Hundred Years of Relativity*. Princeton: Princeton University Press, 2015.

Rossetti, Christina Georgina (1872). *Selected Poems*. London: Penguin, 2008.

Sahakian, William S., and Mabel Lewis Sahakian. *Ideas of the Great Philosophers*. New York: Barnes & Noble, 1966.

Shakespeare, William. *The Complete Works of William Shakespeare (Wordsworth Special Editions)*. London: Wordsworth Editions, 1997.

Spatt, Brenda. *Writing from Sources*. 8th ed. Boston: Bedford/St. Martin's, 2011.

Strunk, William, Jr. and E. B. White. *The Elements of Style*. 4th ed. Boston, Allyn and Bacon, 2000.

BIBLIOGRAPHY

Tolstoy, Leo. (1869). *War and Peace*. New York: New American Library, 1968.
Twain, Mark. *The Adventures of Tom Sawyer*. Chicago, IL: American, 1876.
von Goethe, Johann Wolfgang. *The Sorrows of Young Werther*, ed. Nathen Haskell Dole. Chapel Hill, NC: Project Gutenberg, 2009.
Weldon, Amy E. *The Writer's Eye: Observation and Inspiration for Creative Writers*. London: Bloomsbury, 2018.
Whitman, Walt. *The Complete Walt Whitman* [e-book]. London: Bybliotech, 2012.
Wood, James. *How Fiction Works*. New York: Picador, 2008.

www.ingramcontent.com/pod-product-compliance
Lightning Source LLC
Chambersburg PA
CBHW071710160426
43195CB00012B/1638